The
Gloves are Off

The Gloves are Off

Steve Marsh

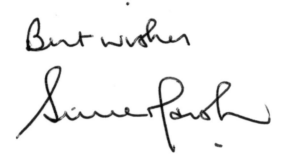

WEST RIDGE

To Mum, Dad, Julie, Hayley and Christian

Acknowledgements
Many thanks to Howard Milton, Mike Gee, Anthony Roberts and
John Evans for their invaluable assistance, and also to Nick Sellens, who
helped bring it all together into some semblance of order!

First published in 2001 by West Ridge Books

ISBN 0-9540733-0-4

Printed and bound in England by
Mackays of Chatham plc

Design and typesetting by Paul Dutnall

Paper kindly supplied by Denmaur Papers Limited

WEST RIDGE BOOKS
16, West Ridge,
Sittingbourne
Kent   ME10 1UJ

Contents

1 Good name for a wicket-keeper   9

2 Learning the ropes   25

3 Marshy? Captain?   45

4 Match of my life   73

5 Four Lord's a weeping   85

6 It's a jungle out there   101

7 Bettin' and Boozin'   123

8 Supporters and Detractors   136

9 Taking stock   148

Career Statistics

Foreword
by **Dickie Bird** MBE

It gives me great pleasure to do the foreword of Steven's book. I remember him starting his career with Kent as a young man, and when I saw him for the first time, I said then he would have a very successful career in cricket. I have been proved right.

Few sportsman achieve the pinnacle of their chosen sport. Despite great effort or outstanding talent the majority of them never make it. They recognise in others the talent they never had and had always hoped for. They play out their dreams through their heroes.

Such experts would have no difficulty in recognising the outstanding talent and application of Steven Marsh, who not only reached the pinnacle of his sport but excelled there.

When you think of all the great wicket-keepers Kent have produced over the years, Les Ames, Hopper Levett, Alan Knott, to name just a few, Steven is up there with them. I can not pay him a higher compliment than that.

Steven as been a fine wicket-keeper, and also a fine captain of Kent who set us all an admirable example.

Steven has had his moments. His contribution has been valuable and characteristic and now is the time to collect the rewards for his endeavours. I wish him well with his autobiography and I hope it will be a tremendous success enjoyed by all cricket lovers.

Dickie Bird.

Introduction

As I've never been short of a few words to say for myself on a cricket field, it will come as no surprise to Kent followers that I've finally got around to committing to paper my perspective on a long and sometimes controversial career.

It has been unfortunate to say the least that my nineteen seasons with the county appear to have coincided with the gradual waning of a once great cricketing colossus. Whatever the rights and wrongs of the last two decades, I believe the collective voice of the players has been largely ignored by the Kent hierarchy, much to the detriment of the club's fortunes both on and off the field. By finally being able to give a player's slant on the relative decline of a fine county club, I hope at the very least to give Kent supporters a keener angle on the root causes of our underachievement.

The major motivation behind writing this book has not been however to lay blame and point fingers. To those individuals who have conspired to shape my career, whether for better or worse, I've tried to be as fair and as honest as possible. I nevertheless make no apologies for ruffling a few feathers where necessary.

In the process of setting the record straight on a number of issues, some contentious, some frivolous, I'll hopefully give a clearer insight into the real personalities that populate cricket. The county game has been wonderful to me over the years and I hope I have succeeded in conveying a sense of the enjoyment and sheer fun of half a lifetime's involvement in this most enthralling of sports.

I'm under no illusion as to how lucky I've been.

ONE

Good name for a wicket-keeper

County aficionados will be doubtlessly disappointed to learn that by virtue of being born at Westminster Hospital on 27th January 1961, I neither qualify as a Kentish man nor as a man of Kent. Indeed Steven Andrew Marsh's association with the county wouldn't commence until a parental decision was made some seven years later to swap the high-rise concrete jungle of West London for the low-rise concrete jungle of Walderslade in the Medway Towns. Traditionalists, however, need not fret. The only vestige of my days as a Londoner is an unhealthy passion for the blues of Chelsea. Otherwise I'm as Pop Larkin as you like!

As is the case with ninety-nine per cent of red-blooded English schoolboys with a hole in their diaries, it was football that first fired my sporting imagination. As a naturally athletic child with a better than average knack of slotting a tennis ball between two proverbial piles of jumpers, I dreamt of becoming Chatham's answer to Peter Osgood, or perhaps even the legendary Mickey Droy! I progressed well through the age groups but as I reached my teens, it was looking increasingly likely that my meagre stature would prevent me from making any real mark on the beautiful game. So instead of making my way westwards up the A2 towards Stamford Bridge, I turned east and ended up leading the line for Whitstable Town in the Kent League for a couple of seasons. It wasn't champagne but at least it was oysters!

As a schoolboy, cricket was nothing more than a bland filling between two crusty slices of football season. Being a lover of all sports, I needed something that would give me competitive involvement over the summer months, so I would tag along with my father to make up the numbers for Lordswood, his local league team. Week after week I would take the "thanks for coming" award as I neither batted nor bowled, being selected merely on the basis of my fielding prowess and metronomic availability.

I had never given the slightest consideration to one day making a living out of football's poor relation. After all, I didn't pick up a cricket bat in anger until I was fourteen! At Walderslade Senior School the sound of leather on willow had long since given way to the thwack of bamboo on trouser. For my contemporaries and me, the noble art of cricket had about as much profile as a pimple on Bernard Manning's backside. So it was one of those fortuitous twists of fate that finally set me along a career path that would span almost twenty years in the professional game. I use the term "twist" advisedly as one man's misfortune, as is so often the case, can become another's gilt-edged opportunity. My break came at Catford while playing for Lordswood seconds. Our wicket-keeper, who was batting at the time, slipped a disc and was stretchered off leaving us with nobody to man the stumps for the home side's innings. Sniffing an opportunity to elbow my way into the action, I thrust my arm up quicker than James Herriot's in calving season. As luck would have it I somehow managed to hang on to four catches - a couple between my legs and one under my chin - and kept hold of the gloves for the next game. So at the almost impossibly late age of fifteen, it was just possible that I'd finally found my sporting niche.

While most cricketers who make it through to the professional ranks do so by going through the system from under tens all the way up, I didn't experience any representative cricket until I played Kent second eleven. It could be suggested that I missed out on the benefits of a structured path to first-class cricket, but I would argue that it was an advantage because I didn't suffer from any baggage of expectation. For many ambitious youngsters in the first echelons of representative cricket, the pressure of maintaining their unforgiving timetable of achievement can be overwhelming.

So to all intents and purposes I slid into wicket keeping via the tradesmen's entrance. No ambitions, no aspirations, no pressure, it just happened that my eager little mug was in the right place at the right time. It was pure, glorious luck that I fell into a specialist position for which I happened to have a natural aptitude. If anyone had told me I'd be one day making several pilgrimages to Lord's, I'd have assumed it was for the purpose of curing some life threatening ailment.

Some people are born to play cricket, some people aspire to play cricket, and others have playing cricket thrust upon them. The fact that I was most definitely in the last bracket gave me the sort of relaxed, uncluttered, pragmatic attitude that undoubtedly hastened my development. I also enjoyed the huge advantage of never having been under any parental pressure. So many fathers these days attempt to live out their sporting fantasies through their offspring and in the process often turn them into psychological wrecks before they are ten. I certainly don't remember my dad straining to chin the umpire if he falsely signalled four byes against me!

At Lordswood, I had progressed from the colts to the second team and finally the firsts when I was asked by George Baker, a former wicket-keeper with the Maidstone-based Kent League team, The Mote, whether I wanted any wicket-keeping coaching. I enthusiastically took him up on his offer and it was during the three seasons I spent at the Maidstone club that I was asked to fill in for the Kent second eleven while then 'keeper, Stuart Waterton, was away at university. On his return after three games I went back to my desk job in London, all the wiser for the experience and totally unaware that my keeping had caught the influential eye of former England opening batsman and acting Kent cricket manager Brian Luckhurst.

Edging towards my twenties, I was still desperately struggling for a bit of direction in my life. I had finished school with a respectable haul of six O-levels and a brace of A-levels but my lack of real vocation had led me to enrol on a vague OND business studies course at Mid-Kent College in Maidstone. With a licence to crunch numbers under my belt I then got an accounts job with the BBC in its foreign travel department. So if you want to know what Kate Adie's knicker allowance was, I'm your man!

Then in the July of 1981 I came home one evening and my parents told me that Kent had been on the 'phone wanting to offer me a second eleven playing contract. So there I was, jaw on the floor, faced with a choice. I could either bide my time at Television Centre and hope to get "spotted" as the Medway Towns' slightly undernourished answer to Noel Edmonds or I could take a bash at making it as a cricketer. The lure of representing my county and thereby escaping a lifetime of stifling bureaucratic mumbo-jumbo was just too tempting and rather unsurprisingly I ended up plumping for "white horse" rather than "White City". I was under no illusions however as to the size of the challenge I was taking on. 'At the moment playing cricket full time means a lot to me but I know it's a long way to go,' I told the *Kent Messenger*, 'I know just how difficult it could be to do it in Kent.'

My four year apprenticeship in the second team was probably a year too long and I gradually found myself getting stale from the lack of top grade competition on which I thrived. Looking back on my team-mates for my first match, it's noticeable how precarious life was for second string players looking to make it through to the first team squad. Of the players who joined the county at roughly the same time as me, only Graham Cowdrey made it through to play regularly in the first team.

With blue cricketing blood coursing through his veins, Graham and I had about as much in common as Prince Charles and Prince Naseem. But despite our differing backgrounds we got on really well and enjoyed each other's sense of fun. Graham has probably got one of the most wicked senses of humour of anyone I know and he was the perfect room mate, although our differing social habits meant that he was usually going out the door just as I was coming in and vice versa! The similarities in our career progression were nicely underlined by the fact we scored maiden first-class centuries on the same day. It was the first four day game after the abolition of three day cricket and we were up at Chelmsford against Essex. On a superb batting wicket Graham and I had a field day and ended up putting on over two hundred. I finished on 120 and Graham got 142. Sadly we hadn't quite got to grips with the new format and declared too early, allowing Essex to rack up six hundred odd!

The fact that we ended up losing the game was in no way going to dampen our celebration. As we were in Brighton that night for a Benson & Hedges game the next day, we decided to go out and crack open a couple of bottles of champagne and polish it all off in time honoured fashion with an Indian. As it happened, the champers took its predictable toll on the virtually teetotal Graham and, when we got back, he nose-dived into his pit and passed out. I too retired but it wasn't long before I woke up with a mouth as dry as Gandhi's flip-flop. I trudged into the bathroom, filled up the tumbler with tap water, slugged it down and went back to bed.

The next thing I knew it was barely getting light and Graham was giving me a vigorous and very unwelcome shake.

'Marshy, Marshy, did you have a drink last night?'

'Cow, I know you don't often drink but you can't have been that pissed, of course I had a drink with you!'

'No, no, you don't understand. Did you have a glass of water?'

'Yeah, I got up in the middle of the night and had a glass of water. What's the matter?'

'Well when I got in I wanted to crash straight out, so instead of putting my contact lenses into their case, I put them into the tumbler in the bathroom with bit of saline solution.'

Then it finally dawned on me - I'd swallowed his bloody lenses! All sorts of unpleasant scenarios ran through my mind, but at least the consumption of a pretty virulent curry the night before should have hopefully ruled out any examination of my lower intestinal area! I certainly wasn't up for going through the motions at that time of the morning.

So Graham was in a predicament. How was he going to face the Sussex quicks without even the end of his bat in focus? There was only one thing to do and he got into his car and drove back to his flat in Canterbury - not a good idea considering he was probably still half-cut and half-blind - to pick up another pair. In the end he made it back with minutes to spare and the crisis was averted.

I related the saga to a freelance journalist I know named Dudley Moore and, weirdly, the story found its way into newspapers in New Delhi and Sydney. Whether their editors were under the impression that they were dealing with the other Dudley Moore, I'm not sure, but I reckon the Cowdrey factor may just have had something to do with it.

Playing for Kent seconds, I still wasn't thinking in terms of a prolonged career in the professional game. Like anyone first starting out I was happy to play for nothing, simply being glad to be there. The fact that at the start of the 1982 season I had become a contracted player was almost an incidental: I was just thrilled to be involved.

In a scenario not unlike the "Shilton or Clemence" conundrum that was facing the then England football manager Ron Greenwood, I found myself occupying the 'keeper's spot on a rotating basis with Stuart Waterton. It was, of course, unacceptable that I would keep for a game and then compulsorily have to give up my place, regardless of my performance. Neither of us was given the opportunity to show what we could do over a run of games and the general lack of continuity doubtlessly had an adverse effect on our development as wicket-keepers, as well as disrupting the make-up of the side. Equally frustrating was the fact we also shared the first team understudy role to Alan Knott, who by then was nearing the end of his long and distinguished career. For a youngster trying to make his way in the first team, it was not easy to accept the vagaries of the squad rotation system - especially when a faultless display of keeping was automatically rewarded by drink tray duty for the next match.

This wholly unsatisfactory arrangement carried on for another three years. It seemed at the time that the Kent hierarchy were always frightened of making wrong decisions, preferring to keep their options open at all times. Of course it was inevitable that the county would occasionally lose a good player, but sometimes in life you have to make a difficult choice and back yourself with that decision. It came to a head in 1985 when there was talk that Knott was about to announce his retirement. Stuart and I went to the committee and suggested that the time had come for them to choose which of us was their preferred option because, if the situation were to continue into the following year, we would both be looking to leave. It wasn't an idle threat as offers from Somerset and Northamptonshire were on the table.

It was my stroke of good fortune that Chris Cowdrey had just taken over the captaincy from Chris Tavaré. I am sure that if the latter had still been in charge, Stuart Waterton would have been named the next Kent wicket-keeper. Tavaré appreciated Stuart's dedication and commitment to the training ethic while Cowdrey liked my exuberance and self-belief, even though I was far more my own person. In the end it was Stuart who made the trip to Northampton. I like to think that the fact that he only played there a couple of seasons before moving on to the minor counties scene justified Chris Cowdrey's hunch that I had what it takes to make it in county cricket. I looked forward to repaying his faith.

On 3rd May 1982, my first-class career got off to a decent start in my debut match against Oxford University at The Parks. Three catches and no byes conceded until after tea seemed to have pleased Mr Luckhurst. 'He kept very tidily,' he told the *Evening Post*, 'he has the right sort of temperament and is confident in his own ability.'

A week later Alan Knott asked to be withdrawn from the side to face Warwickshire in the championship at Dartford as his wife had been admitted to hospital for an operation. My time had come. We batted first and I remember the satisfaction of seeing off Bob Willis as I progressed to a useful if unspectacular contribution of 10 not out. Buoyed by this avoidance of failure, I went out for the last forty-five minutes before stumps and it wasn't long before I felt the elation of my first first-class scalp: a diving catch down the leg-side to dismiss Dennis Amiss off Kevin "Grunter" Jarvis. It was nice to get off the mark in spectacular fashion and the *Daily Express* was particularly enthused, calling it "a catch of which any of Kent's great wicket-keepers would have been proud."

Having ended the first day on a high, I was brought hurtling back to earth on the morning of day two. The great West Indian Alvin Kallicharran had only just come to the crease when he top-edged an attempted sweep off Derek Underwood straight up in the air. Any coach will tell you that the cardinal sin in that situation is to perform the full 360 degree Al Jolson impersonation, which was, of course, exactly what I did! Worried about the stumps being next to me, I completely lost my bearings and ended up diving full length, not even managing to get a glove on the ball. Just to round off this hapless piece of Keystone Kricket, it landed no more than two yards from where I was in the first place. It was the biggest crowd I'd ever played in front of and you could tell from the dull chorus of moans and groans that the consensus was that Knotty would have undoubtedly done a hand-stand, caught the ball between his buttocks and farted it back to the bowler.

Yet in hindsight this calamity was probably one of the best things that could have happened to me. I'd just dropped a relative dolly to dismiss one of the world's great batsmen off one of the world's great bowlers. For a moment, I thought my career was over before it had started, but after a couple of deliveries I took stock of the situation and said to myself that if I was going to let that sort of thing affect me, I might as well pack it all in right away. It may be a notorious cricketing cliché, but to tell yourself "it's history" is one of the most valuable defensive mechanisms you can employ. It's no good tying yourself in knots, if you'll pardon the pun, it's a case of putting the last ball out of your mind and focusing one hundred per cent on the next one.

I needn't have beaten myself up too violently as my championship debut was received positively by the national press. Doug Ibbotson of the *Daily Telegraph* even went so far as to announce "Kent unearth another Marsh"! A little over-the-top perhaps to be compared to my illustrious Australian namesake after ten runs and one catch, but I was flattered nevertheless.

For the remainder of the short time that we played together in the first team, I have to say I didn't find it particularly difficult to keep to Derek Underwood, which I know will surprise a few people. Despite his legendary variation, "Deadly's" utterly dependable accuracy meant that you never had to take too many balls down the leg-side. What's more, if the batsman missed, he'd invariably hit. On a wicket with consistent turn, you could predict exactly what was going to happen, even though he was bowling at a nippy pace. For a right-handed batsman you knew the ball would turn away from the bat and instinctively you'd be there. The difficulty arose, as it does with all left arm spinners, when the wicket would only offer occasional turn. Two or three overs would come through straight and then all of a sudden one would turn and bounce a mile. Obviously when Derek was bowling, it was coming through so quickly that you might miss it.

It was the quicker bowlers who were more likely to leave me with egg on my face. On many an occasion I was made to look a complete clown by pace-men like Graham Dilley who could send down deliveries that would swing and dip prodigiously once they had beaten the bat. Thankfully only certain bowlers possessed this knack and it remains a phenomenon that nobody can properly explain, least of all yours truly!

The best bowler I ever kept wicket to was the Australian Terry Alderman. It was such a pity I was only around for one of the two seasons he spent with us as he was so skilful, I honestly felt he could find the edge at will. He was one of those bowlers who seemed to have the ball on the end of a piece of elastic and it was fantastically vindictive the way he'd tease batsmen with outswingers of varying widths and then fire in a mesmerising in-ducker to either bowl them or trap them helplessly in front shouldering arms. He had to be the most efficient purveyor of the three card trick I'd ever seen. When they were on their mettle, Richard Ellison and Alan Igglesden could bamboozle the best of them, but in terms of posing a constant threat, Terry Alderman was unquestionably number one.

Like some other great bowlers, Terry seemed to perform best when he had a gut load of beer inside him. The more unhelpful he felt the wicket would be, the more blotto he'd get the night before. A particularly flat track was called an "eight pinter" and if you got to the ground early the next morning, you'd generally see Terry jogging round the boundary, trying to run off his previous night's excesses. That's the thing about cricket. You can abuse yourself royally the night before playing and still produce a match-winning performance. I was carefully making mental notes.

It's been said to me on more than one occasion that deputising for a wicket-keeping great like Alan Knott must have been hugely beneficial to my overall development. Unfortunately the reality is that I really didn't have too much to do with Knotty all the while we were together at the club. He seemed to be a guy who either didn't want to give information away or expected me, as a youngster, eager to learn the trade, to go to him. I have always had a belief in my own abilities that has undoubtedly been translated into cockiness in the eyes of quite a few people, and for this reason I generally tended to work on my own game plan.

I was well aware of Kent's fifty year tradition of producing wicket-keepers of outstanding calibre but I refused to be frightened by it. 'After Alan Knott,' I told the *Evening Post*, 'I don't feel there is any pressure on me. I know I have just got to go in and play the way I know and try not to play like Alan Knott - even if that were possible.' My refusal to be fazed by the ghosts of 'keepers past was not lost on Chris Cowdrey. 'Steve's a very mature young man,' said the Kent skipper in June 1986, 'and he can cope with having to follow Alan Knott. I well remember an impressive batting performance by him against Richard Hadlee at Folkestone when he made 48. That innings said a lot about his character and temperament.'

In the knowledge that I'd finally been chosen as Kent's number one wicket-keeper, I spent the winter of 1985/86 playing cricket in Cape Town under the watchful eye of former Kent and England batsman, Bob Woolmer. As well as teaching me better shot selection in my batting, Bob gave me an invaluable insight into the daily rigours of first-class cricket. His breadth of expertise led me to fully appreciate why he's had so much success coaching Warwickshire and the South African test side. Bob is an instinctive man-manager and his ability to assess the motivational requirements of differing personalities taught me valuable lessons which I drew upon when dealing with players as Kent captain some ten years later. Ironically, his season of coaching Kent in the mid-eighties didn't quite work out as he failed to earn the full respect of players he'd been playing with the summer before. He'd had the reputation for occasional pettiness as a player, which incidentally didn't transfer over to his coaching, so it took the blank canvas of Warwickshire for his full potential to be realised.

I was out in the Cape with Alan Igglesden and Yorkshire's Paul Jarvis and we three amigos were contracted to play for a side called Avendale. Being the club's trio of professionals we were given a blue VW Combi van to use as our staff car, which Paul and I drove as we were the only ones who had driving licences. Getting around was therefore not a problem - that was until the day we played a local "Defence" team near Stellenbosch. Luckily they were "defence" by name but not by nature and we ended up having a good, expansive game, accompanied by copious amounts of post-match amber-coloured hospitality. Nicely lagered and with several choruses of "Four and Twenty Voortrekkers" still ringing in our ears, we suddenly found ourselves having to negotiate the 35 miles back to our digs in Sea Point, Cape Town. Paul and I were so absolutely bladdered that we would have lost our licences three or four times over if we'd been stopped. So we then hit on the idea of giving Iggy his first international driving lesson. After all, they drive on the left in SA so where was the problem? OK, Iggy didn't know how to drive and was just as pie-eyed as we were, but it was hardly a case of tackling the M40 junction of the M25 at six o'clock on a Friday night.

So off we trundled, and I have to say, Iggy wasn't making too bad a job of it. Then, just two minutes from home, we encountered a queue of traffic that was snaking up the up the hill in front of us. It was stop-start, stop-start for a couple of minutes and the concentrated hill-start practice was beginning to take its toll on Iggy's composure, our nerves and the VW's gearbox. As nothing was coming the other way, I told him to pull out and overtake so we could snick in home at the top of the hill. Iggy obliged, but three-quarters of the way up, we discovered it was in fact a road block and were confronted by an armed policeman with his arm in the air. To say we were mindful of the less than caring and sharing reputation of the average South African bobby was understating it slightly, but by then Iggy had built up an unstoppable momentum. White knuckles to the fore, we burst through the road block, sending Cape Town's Finest flying in all directions.

In a situation not dissimilar to the bus escape sequence in the film *Where Eagles Dare*, I turned round to see rifles being ranged disconcertingly in our direction. Having got over the brow of the hill I told an ashen-faced Iggy that we had two choices. Either we stop now, give ourselves up and brace ourselves for a good whipping, or we shoot off round the corner to Jarvo's place and scuttle off to hide in his garage. He paused for a second and then jammed into gear for one last excruciating, bone-shuddering time and scooted down a side road and into the garage quicker than a rat up a drainpipe. Paul and I crept out for a recce after a few minutes and, although the coast was clear, a gibbering Iggy refused to emerge for another two and a half hours! He was right to feel a little perturbed as, when a touring Franklyn Stephenson tried a similar stunt, he was mistaken for a local and ended up with bullet holes in his windscreen!

While we were out in South Africa, Iggy wasn't just learning his cricket, he was honing his boozing skills as well. After finishing a coaching clinic one evening we went on to a party just outside Newlands cricket ground. It would turn out to the night Iggy won his drinking spurs. The three of us had already had a good beer-up with the coaches and we arrived at the do totally the worse for wear. Several lager-sodden hours later it was time to go. The bad news was that the booze had obviously permeated each and every cubic millimetre of Iggy's untrained body and he was out cold and immovable. No amount of cajoling, shaking or shouting would even partially stir him, so in the end I had to revert to a good old-fashioned punch on the nose. A quick clunk on the conk seemed to do the trick and he regained just about enough consciousness for us to be able to stuff him into the front passenger seat of the blue Combi.

Unfortunately Iggy isn't one of those things in life that is as reliable as a VW and by the time I'd gone round to get in the driver's side, he'd disappeared. I ran back and found him spread-eagled on the pavement. So I scooped him up one more time and we eventually managed to get back to our place and parked down a side road. As dawn was starting to break, I asked Iggy if he'd got the door keys and he confirmed he had. We then walked up to the house and when I asked him to give me the keys, he changed his mind and said he hadn't got them, they were still in the van. By the time I trotted back from the van some forty yards back in the side road, Iggy had proceeded to climb on top of a neighbour's VW Beetle and was merrily jumping up and down on its roof as if it were a kiddies' bouncy castle! He was yelling and waving at passing motorists and generally behaving like an escapee from the happy farm. I dragged him off the badly crumpled car and bundled him off to bed. By lunchtime he had just about come to and naturally couldn't remember a thing. 'Cor, Marshy', he said, 'I don't know what happened last night, but my nose doesn't half hurt!'

No set of Iggy stories would be complete without reference to his prodigious talent at getting himself injured. In fact he broke down with ailments so often, we really should have nick-named him "Iggy-Stop"! A notable addition to his locker of physical calamities was the time at Tunbridge Wells when he actually managed to twist his ankle tripping over the boundary rope on entering the field of play. There he was, the only man in the history of cricket who had to go off before he came on! But perhaps the most notorious occasion was when we were playing Nottinghamshire at Trent Bridge in the County Championship. Iggy had only just come back from another one of his lay-offs and was really pumped up to rid himself of the perennial sick-note tag. Bowling really well at the top of the innings, Iggy charged in to the wicket one more time. Just as he hit his delivery stride he let out an almighty blood-curdling scream and collapsed as if hit by a sniper's bullet. Mindful of the scenario when Gloucestershire's David Lawrence went down in agony in similar fashion with a split knee-cap playing for England, we collectively swallowed hard and gathered round to survey this potentially career threatening catastrophe. Expecting a ruptured ankle, a collapsed knee or a damaged back we were a little surprised to see him clutching his face. On being asked what the problem was he groaned, 'It's weird. I've never done it before. Just as I threw my arm up in the delivery, I jabbed my thumb straight in my eye'. So deep consternation immediately turned into wholesale hilarity, but it wasn't so funny for Iggy as I think it blinded him for half an hour!

I'm certain cricket would have passed me by if I hadn't been such a weed as a youngster. Always looking four or five years younger than my age, I struggled to make any impression whatsoever on the opposite sex. While my mates spent their mid-teens gallivanting around, steaming up the backs of cars with their eager young consorts, I had little option other than to throw myself into my sport and douse myself under plenty of cold showers. It seemed to take years for my emaciated frame to fill out. I remember when I turned up to enrol at Mid-Kent College aged sixteen, my course colleagues were stunned to learn that I was actually on their course rather than just another snotty school-kid on a day visit! To make it worse, I couldn't get into a pub either. I'd have to sit outside cuddling a coke while my pals were inside living it up. It's obviously why I've spent the rest of my life overcompensating!

The trauma of looking far too young for my years was probably to blame for the acquisition of the Marshy moustache. Obviously some sort of psychological crutch to make me feel a bit more macho, it developed form the original thirsty eyebrow into a Kenny Sansom, before finally thickening into a fully-fledged Tom Selleck. In the mid-eighties it combined with one of my equally hideous shaggy perms to make me look remarkably like an anaemic Lionel Richie. But despite all my initial insecurities, I quickly made up all the lost ground and in 1983 I finally met Julie, my future wife.

I was just about to start my third year as a pro when I was in a Gillingham club getting in some pre-season drinking practice. I was strutting around as usual when I tripped over a step and sent myself flying like a shot of red-eye across the length of a table full of girls on a hen night. With my carefully constructed aura of cool shattered, I decided, like all good chancers, to twist the situation to my advantage. So I rolled over, looked up at the attractive brunette, under whose nose I had come to rest, and made my play. 'May I have the next dance?' I ventured.

With the ice having been broken so sensitively we engaged in the usual "and what do you do?" banter. She appeared a little crest-fallen when I told her that I was unemployed, but perked up when I said that in the summer I was a cricketer.

'Who do you play for then?' she inquired, strangely inquisitive.

'Well actually it's Kent', I responded with a "now pick that out the net" air of smugness. Julie then trumped my trump in a bravura moment: 'That's funny, my father's on the Kent committee!'

Of all the gin-joints in all the towns in all the world, the daughter of a Kent committee member walks into mine. It turned out that Julie's father was Bob Wilson, the prolific Kent batsman of the late fifties and sixties. She did go back and ask him whether he knew of my existence but, in true committee fashion, he told her he'd never heard of me!

Julie and I got married in September 1986, shortly after I had been awarded my county cap. A year that had started out with a mixture of excitement and apprehension turned out to be a watershed in the life of Steve Marsh. With 800 first-class runs under my belt and 50 dismissals, I'd arrived both as a man and a cricketer. In trying to replace the irreplaceable Alan Knott, I'd faced what Brian Luckhurst called "the hardest job in cricket" and had somehow survived. I had a funny feeling however, the hardest part was yet to come.

TWO

Learning the ropes

It was daunting to be now sharing a dressing-room with some of the greats of the modern game. Asif, Knott, Underwood...Marsh! It was like Darren Day trying to gate-crash a Rat Pack concert. However I comforted myself in the knowledge that these deities also had to eat, sleep and break wind, so why should they intimidate me?

Luckily it never came to that as the atmosphere in the Kent dressing-room was always warm, welcoming and genial. But although I was a chirpy and confident young player, I made sure I kept my thoughts to myself so I didn't encroach on their domain. In the early days, my job was to look and learn.

The players with whom I most readily identified were the jokers in the pack: Bob Woolmer and the two Grahams, Dilley and Cowdrey. Bob made me chuckle because his humour, despite being unbelievably childish, was wonderfully infectious. When your knackers were greeted by the very individual Deep Heat sensation when you pulled on your scants, Bob was usually the culprit. Without doubt Graham Cowdrey was the club comedian and constantly had us in stitches. His impressions were brilliantly observed. He did a superb Robin Smith, but my favourite had to be his Mohammad Azharuddin. Azharuddin always wore a small black leather pouch around his neck and I once looked out over the balcony at Northampton during a rain interval and saw Graham wiggling his bat in the air shouting "one more, thank you very much", with his head poking through the loops of a large black sports bag!

The joking around was by no means confined to the dressing-room. Out in the middle I took great delight in generating a juicy piece of flatulence in an attempt to distract the batsman at the critical moment. You could only do it when a spinner was bowling because if you were keeping to someone like Martin "Macca" McCague, the effort required to carry the noise thirty yards back to the batsman could leave you playing on a very sticky wicket. The secret was to time your effort so it coincided with the bowler bringing his front foot down onto the crease. He'd be giving it a rip at one end and I'd be letting rip at the other! Occasionally I'd have a bit of a problem with my follow-through but at least it made the slips laugh.

The mickey-taking was pretty much shared around, but the one person we could never lay a glove on was Neil Taylor. Neil had a very dry sense of humour and had an armoury of acidic comments effective enough to cut any would-be joker down to size. He was due some retribution, however, as he was notoriously shy about buying drinks. He was so bad that the guys christened him "Crime", because, as we all know, "Crime" doesn't pay. As he was impervious to verbals, we decided to wind him up by taking a pot of glue to his footwear at Leicester one afternoon. Trevor Ward immediately volunteered to do the dirty work and grabbed a broom handle to wedge one of Neil's shoes up against the dressing-room ceiling. Neil, who'd been watching TV in one of the other rooms, strolled back in and caught him red-handed with his usual impeccable timing. This particular shoe was now most definitely on the other foot and Trevor was mortified.

'Trevor,' questioned Neil, giving his victim the full Anne Robinson treatment, 'what do you think you are doing?'

'Ah, oh, err....look Crime,' wittered Wardy, completely bang to rights, 'it wasn't me, honest!'

'What are you talking about, Trevor? You're standing there with my shoe on the end of a broom handle!'

'Er...yeah...but, I didn't *want* it to be me!'

And so it went on. We could never get him!

In terms of temperament, Wardy was at one end of the spectrum and Chris Tavaré was at the other. Tav didn't know the meaning of the word emotion. He would have cleaned up at poker because his demeanour and routine in the dressing-room never altered one iota. After his innings he'd stroll in, open up his coffin and methodically place each item of kit in its allotted place. You'd never have known whether he'd just been triggered first ball or blasted a double ton.

By comparison, Trevor was a psychotic. When Wardy got out, the standard drill was for the dressing-room to be evacuated in double time. I've never known anyone be so uptight. If the degree of injustice or stupidity of his dismissal was sufficient, he would storm back in shouting 'I don't know why I bother playing this effing game, I'm effing useless, I might as well commit effing suicide' and launch his bat half-way across the room, bouncing it off four walls. I've got to say I found it all hilarious. Most of the time I'd have to be padding up when Wardy was out so I'd always be sitting there chuckling under my breath, and even if I wasn't, I'd come in especially!

It was also amusing to watch his feathers get ruffled when the crowd started to get on his back for slow scoring. Trevor took particularly unkindly to sarcastic applause if he was struggling to find his form and he would routinely raise his arms and wave his bat in the air in fury as if to beckon the culprits out into the middle for a fight!

It was such a pity that he was beset by these demons as I would probably class Trevor as the biggest unfulfilled talent that I ever played with. When he was on song, his timing and shot-making were such that you couldn't bowl at him. But while he had the style and ability to outshine his contemporaries, Graham Thorpe, Mark Ramprakash and Nasser Hussain, the fragility of his temperament, as I'm sure he would freely admit himself, was his downfall time and time again.

Despite his foibles, Wardy was a good lad to have around the place, although his occasionally alarming propensity for gullibility made him prime wind-up fodder! The moment chosen for his initiation into the crazy world of Marsh and Cowdrey was his debut match against Hampshire at Southampton. Trevor was a little worried that his first game would see him facing the fearsome Malcolm Marshall but he got through the ordeal exceptionally well, despite coming back peppered in bruises. Not wishing him to get too carried away with his success I decided to give him a Sunday morning "wake-up" call. I dusted off my best home counties accent and dialled his line.

'Oh good morning Trevor', I oozed, 'my name is Peter O'Toole and I am from Hampshire Schools Cricket. Congratulations on your debut.'

'Oh, thanks very much.'

'I think you stood up to Malcolm very well. I suppose he was bowling pretty fast?'

'Coo yeah, fastest I've ever faced!'

'Well I'll tell you what it is. In the past when Kent have come down we've had people like Nigel Felton and Richard Ellison come along and present the annual Hampshire Schools trophies. Well I was just wondering if you would do us the honour this year by making the presentation. It's tonight at eight o'clock in the Portsmouth cub scout hut.'

Perhaps understandably, Trevor didn't sound too keen.

'Err, well, err, it's a bit far.'

'We will of course refund your petrol and give you directions. We'll also provide some sandwiches, so you needn't worry about eating.'

But he still wasn't convinced.

'Err, well, I'm not sure. I don't think I'll be allowed.'

'Oh I see. Who is it that will decide?'

'Well, I'll tell you what, I'll go and have a word with the captain, Chris Cowdrey.'

'Oh right, fine, I'll give you a call back in a quarter of an hour.'

Well it couldn't have worked out better because, as Graham and I were in the next door room, we were the ones he chose to come in and bleat to. It was a feat of mammoth will-power requiring the facial muscles of a gnu but we both managed to keep straight faces.

'You'll never guess what,' confided Trevor in semi-exasperation, 'I've had some bloke on the 'phone from Hampshire Schools and he wants me to present some prizes at a scout hut in Portsmouth.'

'You're having a laugh,' I replied, poker faced but suppressing a titter, 'I take it you told him no way!'

'Well I tried to but he was pretty persistent. I told him I'd go and ask Chris Cowdrey.'

'That's no problem then,' I said reassuringly, 'when he rings back just tell him Chris said you couldn't go.'

Re-energised with this master-plan, Trevor chirped 'Good idea' and went back purposefully to his room. Naturally I got straight back on the 'phone.

'Ah hello, Peter O'Toole here again. Trevor, I've got some great news! I've managed to get hold of Chris Cowdrey and he told me he thought it was a wonderful idea.'

'W-What?' replied a heart-broken Ward, 'Oh. Err, well, to tell the truth it's a bit far and I don't really want to go all the way out there....'

'But we've had people like Richard Ellison come over from your county...'

'Yeah, but I don't really want to go on my own and....'

I then decided to get shirty. 'I tell you what Trevor, I know people like you and all you want to do is take from the game. You just don't want to give anything back, do you? I suppose you'd rather go out and get pissed!'

Wardy then really bit. 'You what?', he barked, 'I don't even drink! Are you trying to get aggressive with me?'

'No I'm not but I don't like your attitude. I congratulated you on your innings and now to be honest, I'm having regrets about that.'

'Well that's fine,' snapped Trevor, 'I ain't turning up and that's it', and slammed the 'phone down.

He duly came back into our room and he was not a happy chappy.

'That bastard! He reckons people like me just take from the game and give nothing back, I can't believe it...'

'Well if I were you,' piped up Graham, 'I'd ring that Mr O'Toole back and give him a piece of my mind!'

Trevor concurred vehemently. 'Yeah, damn right, I'm gonna...', and then all of a sudden he finally caught the whiff of a large brown rodent, 'hang on a minute, how do you know his name's Mr O'Toole?!'

I could have called myself Omar Sharif and still have got away with it such was his credulity on occasions!

Another guy who'd believe anything you told him was my old oppo from Lordswood, Kevin "Hoddy" Masters, David's father. He'd only just joined the Kent staff and we were travelling down to Wales for a second team game. We'd got to about five miles from the Severn Bridge when the team manager, Colin Page, turned around and said, 'OK guys, we're nearly at the bridge now. Can you all get your passports ready.'

'What, Manage?' inquired Kevin in his usual rough 'n' ready sort of way, 'You never fuckin' told me I gotta bring me passport?!'

'Come on Hoddy,' insisted Colin, 'you know every time you go to Wales, you've got to bring your passport!'

'Ah, fuckin' 'ell,' huffed Hoddy, all crest-fallen and forlorn, 'what am I gonna do then?'

The poor bloke was obviously petrified at the thought of missing his first away game, so Pagey made a suggestion.

'There's a cover at the back of the bus. Go and throw it over yourself and hide behind the back seat.'

He duly obeyed orders and eventually re-emerged drenched in sweat and covered in grime some forty-five minutes later!

Staying in hotels for four or five nights every other week is a hazard of being a professional cricketer and players come to terms with it in different ways. Some manage to fill their spare time better than others, but occasionally the only way to alleviate the boredom is to collectively step out of yourselves and behave like overgrown children. Every county side has its resident pranksters and, at Kent, Graham Cowdrey and I were chairmen of the board. The best victims were normally those who took themselves a little bit too seriously. Despite his privileged background and huge wealth, it would be a little unfair to put Matthew "Jazzer" Fleming in this category, but Graham and I didn't miss the opportunity to stitch him up a treat during one game at Edgbaston. Kicking our heels at the hotel after a day's play with nothing much happening, Graham invited him over to our room for a game of cards. It was never a bad idea to get Jazzer along for a game of brag because if you got dealt a prile, there was a good chance you'd be able to win half of Cornwall off him! After an hour or so he got up for a royal wee, which was the cue for Graham to suggest it was time to have a bit of fun. I was, as always, game and in no time we had hatched a plot that would involve Graham asking Mr Fleming if he could use the 'phone in his room to call his fiancée Maxine. Once there, Graham would unhitch some plastic out of Matthew's body-belt of credit cards and order him up a couple of hookers! Well it all worked like clockwork. Jazzer obligingly gave Graham his key and the furtive nod and wink I got from him as he came back into the room some ten minutes later suggested that the trap had been successfully laid.

Jazzer was up for the game to go on and on but Graham then pretended he was tired so we had an excuse to usher him back to his room. Having got rid of him we both then darted down in the lift to reception so we could observe the arrival of the ladies in question. After fifteen minutes the two of them duly tipped up and, in an operation of breath-taking and obviously well-rehearsed stealth, they eased themselves, virtually unnoticed, from the back entrance over to the lift. We scuttled out from our cover and followed them up in the next lift. We hid behind a corner and waited like naughty schoolboys for contact to be made.

They knocked on the door and Jazzer, sounding more than a little ruffled, assured them he hadn't ordered any room service and refused to come to the door. The girls persisted and eventually he opened up. From our angle it was difficult to make out whether this former army officer was standing to attention or not.

'I think there's been some terrible mistake', he gasped in his clipped Etonian tones as he was greeted by the sight of not one but two pretty young women of relaxed virtue.

Their husky response of 'But Mr Fleming, you booked us using your credit card!' finally caused the penny to drop and when we heard the roar of 'Cowdrey! Marsh!' we knew we were in for it!

He then politely asked the girls to wait and he hurtled down the corridor to our room and started banging on the door demanding that we showed ourselves. Catching sight of a scarpering Graham he then chased him up four flights of stairs. So much for his army training because this particular search and locate mission was a total failure. Nevertheless, true to the officers' code, he requested that the girls stay until Graham had come back to apologise. Eventually Graham did come back down and after the five of us had reconvened in our room, Jazzer asked him to do the decent thing.

'Graham, will you apologise to these two young ladies?'

Graham half chuckled and replied, 'Jaz, these aren't "young ladies", they're hookers!'

With no apology forthcoming, an acutely embarrassed Graham then went and locked himself in the bathroom and refused to come out. The joke was now beginning to back-fire on poor Mr Cowdrey. The girls by now were now starting to enjoy themselves and began to plead with Graham to come out for some "fun". Having summoned up as much bravado as he could, Graham then flung open the door of the bathroom and announced 'Come on girls. I'm ready. What have you got in mind!' To his horror one of them purred 'Oh whatever you want sir!' Graham, in a fashion so typical of a young man with too many years of private school education under his belt, capitulated with a pitifully repressed 'Oh, no, ha-ha, no, no, err, oh Christ, somebody get me out of here!' It was none too impressive. Ever the gentleman, Jazzer escorted them to the lifts and gave them a tip for wasting their time. He hadn't been best pleased but I think he could see the funny side...eventually!

It was definitely a sort of comfortable routine rooming with Graham. He knew my idiosyncrasies and I knew his - not that we were in the room at the same time that often. In fact Graham often said that rooming with me was like having a room to himself. Occasionally, though, we'd arrive a bit late and all the twin rooms would be taken. The thought of having to share with someone like Macca, whose notoriously thunderous snoring brought him the nickname "Rhino", was quite unacceptable if any form of sleep was required, so we'd usually have to concoct a plot to persuade somebody to vacate their room for us. One evening at Taunton, we were mischievously successful at evicting Hartley Alleyne.

Having arrived late and with no twins available, we asked reception for the rooming list and saw that Hartley was on his own. "H" was a good lad and would make a very suitable candidate for our cunning plan. I selected another voice from my portfolio of accents and got on the 'phone.

'Ah hello. Is that Mr Allenne?'

'ALL*EYNE*, man, ALL*EYNE*!'

'Ah, terribly sorry Mr Alleyne, it's reception here. There seems to be some misunderstanding with the rooming list. We had actually pre-booked your room for a married couple that we've got arriving. It's totally our mistake, Mr Alleyne, but if you'd like to pack all your kit up and come down to reception, we'll find you another room.'

Hartley was not impressed. 'Aw, hey man, I'm unpacked and totally relaxed here. I got me pint o' Guinness!'

'Well Mr Alleyne, it wouldn't look too good if a married couple came along and had to have separate rooms, would it?'

Anyway, he finally agreed and we went up and walked past his room. He had the door open and I stuck my head in and said 'Hi "H", how's it going?'

'Aw, man, you never guess what's happenin' here', he complained, with his Guinness in one hand and his bag in the other, 'they want me to move 'cos some married couple are comin' in here or sumfin'. Graham and I already had our kit with us and as he walked out, we walked straight in!

Hartley then went down to reception and found that they'd got no other room for him! He came back up to find us two grinning cuckoos in his nest but could do nothing more than wave an admonishing finger in our direction, 'You bad men, you bad men!'

Another guy to be served an eviction order was Richard Ellison, but this time it was from the Edgbaston dressing-room! Graham and I used to like to spread the action around and one lazy morning before the afternoon's Sunday League game we decided to have a little bit of a laugh at the expense of Kent's shaggy-mopped answer to The Electric Light Orchestra's Jeff Lynne. This time Graham got on the blower and called through to Elly's room.

'I'd like to speak to Chris Cowdrey please.'

'No, no, it's not Chris Cowdrey, it's Richard Ellison.'

'Ah, terribly sorry. I wonder if you could pass a message onto Chris. It's Warwickshire Cricket Club here and we have a slight problem.'

'Oh yeah?'

'Well I'm afraid that the wicket for today's game is right in front of the home dressing-room and the sight screens will also have to be moved. Naturally the Warwickshire players won't be able to see, so we'd like to move them into your dressing-room and offer Kent alternative changing facilities on the far side of the ground. So if you wouldn't mind getting all your kit together...'

'That's a bit out of order isn't it?

'Well I appreciate that, but as Warwickshire are the home team, I'm afraid their requirements must take precedence.'

Never one to rock the boat, Elly agreed to pass on the message to the rest of the team that all our gear had to be decamped. At breakfast he wandered from player to player advising them of the tiresome new arrangements while Graham and I followed on behind informing them that a wind-up was in operation. In the knowledge that he had plenty of packing to do, Elly left to go to the ground early. By the time we'd arrived at the Edgbaston car park he was waddling past us so loaded down by his coffin and bags that he looked as if he'd just waved goodbye to mummy and daddy on his first day at prep school. Like an orphaned pelican in a wildlife documentary, he shuffled off in search of his non-existent nest.

'See you soon Elly,' I chirped reassuringly, 'we'll be over in a minute!' With that we scooted off cackling to the dressing-room and got changed. Twenty minutes later Elly reappeared, dragging his kit laboriously towards us as we warmed up on the outfield. 'Alright then,' he griped doing a remarkable impersonation of Blakey from *On the Buses*, 'which one of you bastards was it then?'

I felt insulted that he needed to ask!

Elly suffered from a particular complaint that made him an absolute nightmare to room with. It could have been fatally illustrated when we were staying at the Grand Hotel in Brighton during an indoor six-a-side tournament. We came nowhere in the competition, but as it had all been just a bit of light-hearted fun and, as our wives were down with us, we thought we'd go out for a celebration anyway. So Iggy, Richard and I plus our other halves went out and had a great evening at a nearby Mexican. In the click of a castanet it was time to vamoose and we meandered our way out all the better for several bottles of tequila. Having made the obligatory appearance at a club we eventually retired after a night-cap at the hotel.

Next morning at breakfast, Fiona, Elly's wife came down and told us that Richard had been up to one of his alcohol-induced sleep-walking tricks again. It had turned out that this time he'd wandered out of his room onto the fire escape. On getting out into the cold night air, the fire escape door shut itself automatically behind him and he woke up to find himself teetering on the edge of the staircase, stark gonad naked!

Brighton on a chilly Saturday night is probably not the optimum location for a red-blooded male to be stranded with his tackle out and Elly's options had shrunk considerably. With the way back barred, he had no other choice than to gingerly make his way down the fire escape and make a run for it through reception back to his room, hopefully being mindful of the lift doors.

The night porter looked on in disgust as the former England seamer sprinted across reception, grabbed a newspaper to protect the crown jewels and hared up the stairs to his room. From that moment on, he wouldn't need any convincing that Elly could indeed swing it both ways!

He used to terrify some of his room mates and his constant sleep-walking and hollering out of windows in the middle to the night meant it wasn't long before he was confined to solitary on a permanent basis!

Believe me, the trappings of fame are not an issue for your average county cricketer. The "cult of personality" developed to a certain extent on the test scene and ebullient, good-looking superstars like Shane Warne are now instantly recognisable outside of the cricketing context. I even saw recently that the fragrant Anna Kournikova has got a soft spot for Darren Gough. Could you imagine Mike Hendrick or Chris Old getting a shine off someone like her twenty years ago?

When it comes to county cricketers, most people couldn't tell their Irani from their Windows, so for most of the time it was a good idea to leave your ego at home tucked up with a nice hot water bottle. That's not to say you can walk around totally unrecognised. There are seven thousand Kent members, so if you accept that the county has a population of about a million, there was technically a one in 142 chance of being tapped on the shoulder in the paper shop. But after a while, your face does start to get recognised and occasionally you get asked to sign the odd autograph for some member's "nephew". Probably the best way of getting yoursef known is to put plenty of miles on your sponsored car, one of a county cricketer's few worth-while perks. Having my name splashed across my car definitely "encouraged" people to put my face to the name, though on the downside, it's a little disheartening when you can lip-read other motorists saying "Steve who?" as you trundle by in your Dagenham rep-mobile. Another bane of a sponsored car is that you can tend to get noticed wherever you go, with people often coming up and saying 'Oh I saw you the other day at so and so', to which I reply 'How the hell did you know I was over there?' So for the first couple of years it was a great way of letting people know you'd "arrived", but after a while I have to say I longed for the anonymity of a scribble-free set of wheels!

So while they save you a lot of money, there are indeed plenty of pitfalls to the perk of driving a sponsored car. I was travelling back down from the north one bank holiday Monday when I met an enormous queue of traffic waiting to file into the Dartford Tunnel. Minding my own business with the windows wound down I was overtaken by a group of guys in a Sierra. They'd obviously thoroughly enjoyed their annual day out to Canvey Island and were clearly much the better for a vat or two of Stella. One of them, can of lager in hand, leaned out of the back window and shouted across to me.

'Oi, Steve, how ya doin' mate?!'

He was obviously from that celebrated school of urchin that amuses himself by driving past cricket grounds screaming "owzat!" but I nevertheless raised my hand in recognition and thanked him graciously for the name-check.

But I could see he hadn't finished and I braced myself for the Ivor Novello moment.

'Steve, I jus' wanna say, I've sin all yer films an' I fink yer brilliant!'

Now that wasn't bad.

A mate of mine, the ex-Gillingham and Peterborough striker

Jason Lillis, also made some sparkling new acquaintances through his sponsored car. One night in Chatham, he'd stopped at a set of traffic lights and a car pulled up alongside. The driver looked over and made a twirly hand gesticulation, inviting him to wind down his window. Obligingly Jason hit the button in anticipation of satisfying some young man's autograph request.

'Are you Jason Lillis?'

'Yeah, that's right.'

'You're that wanker who plays for Gillingham, i'n't ya!'

In the current era of road rage, driving a garishly appointed sponsored car can also be a liability. I have to confess that each time I've been consumed by the red mists, I have the unfortunate tendency to forget that my name and occupation are splashed all over my paintwork in twelve inch high letters.

I was once late for a game at Canterbury and was starting to get rather irate at some of the clueless dodderers who were blocking my progress. On the ring road, a few minutes from the ground, a couple pulled out in a car in front of me and refused to move out of the way. Incensed, I leaned over and gave the gentleman in question a very sharp dose of vitriol before haring off in the outside lane. Macca, who was in the car with me, then confided a disconcertion observation, 'Marshy, I'm pretty sure those two are Kent members. I see them at every game!' Whoops!

Not everyone is quite so politely inquisitive to make the acquaintance of county cricketers. There is a certain type of angry young man who resents what he perceives as your cushy, pampered lifestyle and targets you for abuse. I remember one occasion, after a championship game at Worcester, when some of the team had gone out for a couple of wind-down drinks in the town. Three of us had just left a night club when we were approached by a slurring young inebriate who felt he needed to share with us his thoughts on the meaning of life. I'm not sure whether he knew who we were, but it sounded like he was muttering "Kent" every so often, so I reckon he must have had an idea we were cricketers. Noticing that he was accompanied by a couple of husky lager goddesses, I made the unwise decision of rising to the bait and reciprocating his banter.

'Oh I get it...' I ventured, 'you're obviously looking to show off to your two young lady friends. Sadly, it doesn't look as if they're too impressed, does it girls?'

Pleasingly the two young things nodded their agreement but then, out of the blue, I felt a hefty blow to the side of my head. Three young lads then scarpered with myself, Julian Thompson and Dave Fulton in hot pursuit. Eventually we managed to corner our prey, but only in an area that seemed to be populated by half the Hereford & Worcester constabulary. They tried their utmost to provoke me into hitting them, but I fortunately took Julian's sensible advice and backed off and retired to the hotel. Back in the room, I showered and surveyed the damage to find that I been cut, no doubt by a ring, under my left eye. Fortunately for me, our then coach, Daryl Foster, was wise enough to understand, probably through being an Australian, that these things occasionally happen. So when I turned up the next day in trepidation at the reception my two black eyes would receive, all he did was to chuckle and say 'Whose wife was she then Marshy?'

In the winter months it was just a case of "getting by". Apart from my season in South Africa, I spent every close season of my career poncing a few odd jobs here and there, trying to keep the wolf from the door and somehow maintain my gallivanting lifestyle. It was hardly glamorous though. While the England boys were getting stuck into the local hospitality in various exotic tour locations, I'd be putting my Mid-Kent College training to use again by punching holes in invoices in the accounts department at Swale Motors in Sittingbourne. Actually, it would be most ungracious of me to moan about that particular dealership as my contact there would always make sure I wasn't short of transport over the winter. Other companies used to be yanking car keys off players as soon as stumps were pulled on the last game of the season!

Another of my off-season distractions was a job with a credit check company called Infocheck. It was based in the sumptuous grounds of Godmersham Park near Ashford, the stately home where, so they tell me, Jane Austen wrote *Pride and Prejudice*. With Graham Cowdrey, Chris Penn, Iggy and me on board, it must have quickly become obvious to our benevolent Kent-supporting MD that he hadn't employed too much sense and sensibility. We didn't do a lot of work, took plenty of long lunches and settled back and enjoyed the scenery. Just the ticket.

Financially, life got tougher in 1987 when Julie left her job at the NatWest (and the subsidised mortgage) when she became pregnant with our first child, Hayley. The purse strings were already pretty tight and it was vital that I cultivated the sympathetic ear of the bank manager. One of the many hazards of being a county cricketer is the annual struggle to compensate for the boom and bust cycle of only being salaried for the summer months. The trick was to put something by during the season and then apply for an overdraft to plug the hole in your bank balance until your contract resumed the following April. You'd then be paying off your overdraft for the first half of that season and so it would continue. Every year you'd go back cap in hand and hope that the bank manager's natural scepticism about your reliability would be overcome by the prospect of him getting his sticky mits on a nice, juicy benefit fund ten or so years down the line. For the archetypal county foot-slogger such as myself, the prospect of a lucrative, tax-free benefit year offered a teasing glimpse of financial salvation. If you kept your form and stayed fit, you'd be in with a shout. As a rule of thumb, you were granted a benefit ten years after being capped. However, I cunningly spotted that there was a potential log-jam of eager candidates in the late nineties so I applied a year early. Fortunately, the committee deemed that I had been a good enough boy and in 1994 they sent me a letter confirming to me that the following season was to be my testimonial year.

I know a lot of people who begrudge cricketers their benefit years. Why should some loafer get paid a very handsome tax-free lump sum, when all he's done is chase a little red lump of leather around the playing fields of England with the sun on his back for a dozen or so years? Why don't far more deserving cases like nurses, firemen or teachers qualify for such privileged treatment? Granted, it would be lovely if more professions could reward long-term service in a similar fashion but, for many cricketers, a benefit season remains an all-too elusive perk that barely compensates for the meagre rewards of the intervening seasons.

All players understand that if they serve their county for a certain number of years, they will be entitled to a benefit. Benefits can't be written into players' contracts as they would then be taxable, so the semantics deem that they have to be "granted". On the basis that there could be a medium-sized pot of gold at the end of the rainbow, counties feel they can get away with offering players derisory contract terms. They lock players in on miserly salaries and rolling short-term contracts, knowing that any professional would be loathe to move counties for fear of missing out on their bonanza season. If I'd been six years through my Kent career and another county had come in and offered me a forty per cent increase on my salary, I'd have been very tempted, but I would have had no option but to stay put because the lure of a large tax-free windfall in four years' time would have been simply too great.

On the outside, the counties may appear to be benevolently paternalistic, but in reality they wash their hands of their responsibilities to their players. It's use and abuse all the way down the line. The counties only contribute a small proportion to the final pot. They'll offer a percentage of the receipts of the season's dedicated benefit match, but the bulk of the total will be funded out of the goodness of the supporters' hearts, whether from donations at matches or the organised benefit events. In effect, supporters are paying twice for their cricket and the county committees are laughing all the way to the bank.

Even for beneficiaries who have been fortunate enough to bank a tidy sum, there's no guarantee that the Chancellor won't at some stage demand his pound of flesh. Because some high profile cricketers have recently declared bumper benefits of over £300,000, the tax man's nose has suffered an unfortunate realignment. If a move is made to plug the loophole and benefits are deemed to be taxable income, the Exchequer will be entitled to take its cut retrospectively from any benefit pool generated over the previous seven years. Over one hundred players will suddenly find themselves saddled with a rather large and hugely sobering liability. It's why you'll find that most cricketers announce somewhat "seasonally adjusted" benefit totals.

Of course, not all players will get a benefit. Your heart goes out to fellow pros who loyally give their county nine years of unstinting service, only to miss out on pay-back time when injury prematurely curtails their career. Just look at Dean Headley. There have been few more popular and hard-working servants for Kent over the years than Deano, but his failure to win his battle with his back problem means that he's going to miss out. Neither is it a certainty that Paul Nixon will get a benefit. At the age of twenty-nine he took the gamble of forfeiting a benefit at Leicestershire in order to try and kick-start his career by coming to Kent. By the time his benefit becomes due, not only might his career already be over, but the whole system could have been dismantled anyway.

In net terms, the average county cricketer would probably be better off if benefits were scrapped altogether. The resultant freedom of movement would translate into significantly more bargaining power as counties vied for the top players' signatures. Once players realised that they were perhaps one good season away from a big money transfer with a juicy signing on fee, I'm positive that the overall standard of English county cricket would improve dramatically. While it's definitely in the long-term interests of the game, it's going to be hideously unfair to pull the rug from under the feet of players with eight or nine seasons under their belt.

Any cricketer who's had a benefit will tell you they're damned hard work and almost a full-time job in their own right. Bowlers probably have more time to devote to their benefits as their careers are generally slightly shorter, meaning that by the time their turn comes, they're often either inactive through injury or have been put out to grass in the seconds. It wasn't quite like that for me as I was in the process of taking over the reigns of captaincy from Mark Benson and approaching the peak of my career. At the time it was a distraction I could have possibly done without as the administrative and organisational burden in assembling a year-long programme of events was definitely detrimental to my cricket. I'd be out in the middle keeping wicket and I'd suddenly remember that I hadn't 'phoned a caterer. I would be standing there panicking about vol-au-vents for the rest of the session!

Talking of panic, I almost had kittens at the biggest event of the year, at the Connaught Rooms in London. I'd managed to wangle Rory Bremner as guest speaker for the most prestigious of my benefit dinners and it promised to be a fantastic evening. There are few bigger pulls on the after dinner circuit than Mr Bremner and the assembly room was sold out and buzzing. Rory, who had very kindly waived his fee as a favour, had advised me that other commitments before and afterwards meant he wouldn't be able to make it in time for the 7.30 sit-down. In the end we agreed he could pitch up at 8.45, do his spiel and then slip off again into the night. "An evening with Rory Bremner" had suddenly become "Two cups of coffee and an After Eight mint with Rory Bremner", but as far as I was concerned it didn't represent a problem.

Half past eight came and went and a few of my friends started piping up about Rory's whereabouts. 'Don't worry', I grinned back reassuringly, 'he's got a few things to sort out and he'll be along in a few minutes.' Thirty minutes later and still no show. Had he been pulled over for impersonating a police officer? With the waitresses clearing dessert courses with almost indecent haste I asked them to go easy on the coffees while I figured out which chandelier I had to swing from to escape a possible lynching. Some of the more sadistic smart-arses in my so-called circle of friends were starting to revel in my increasing despair. A menu was sent over to me with "an evening *without* Rory Bremner" scrawled across it, and then another with "an evening with *Billy* Bremner". I emitted a horrendously forced chuckle but it was a totally unconvincing attempt at nonchalance. Then, just as I was about to stand up and regale the £250 a head punters with half an hour of Steve Marsh's all-time best Iggy stories, I finally got the nod that Rory had arrived and was outside and raring. That half an hour of hell is not something I ever want to endure again but the excellence of Rory's performance at least made my angst all worth while...just.

Matthew Fleming's also a very good speaker and he was kind enough to say a few words for me at a ladies' lunch. Ninety-eight per cent of the women there thought he was hilarious, but shortly afterwards I had a couple of letters from one or two Lady Bracknells complaining about the bluish tint of some of his jokes. 'I was absolutely disgusted with Matthew Fleming,' harangued one correspondent, 'When I heard he was speaking I was thrilled and was looking forward to hearing stories of his days at Eton and the Royal Green Jackets. All we got was smut!'

The distractions of my benefit year definitely took their toll on my on-field performances, but in the broader context of giving me and my family a firm financial foundation on which to build, it was a minuscule price to pay. While I'm in no position to decamp permanently to the golf course, my benefit year certainly enhanced my lifestyle and with luck I'm still a few years off having to apply for the Rodmersham *Big Issue* franchise. I just hope that in the coming years a sensible remuneration structure is put in place that will allow cricketers to avoid this lottery.

THREE

Marshy? Captain?

There are two basic styles of captaincy: the cerebral and inspirational. During my career I played under both scholarly introverts and gregarious live-wires and my eventual core philosophy on the game became a blend of these two extremities.

I didn't pick up much however from my first skipper, Asif Iqbal. In the year or so that our careers overlapped, he probably said no more than a dozen words to me: "how are you", "well batted", "did you know there's a caterpillar on your top lip?", and so on. He'd waft in and out in his pleasant but imperious way and you'd hardly see him from one week to the next.

Next up after Asif was Chris Tavaré. Tav had a good cricketing brain and was very astute but he never inspired me. Though I liked him as a guy, he wasn't able to fire my imagination and I ended up having to generate my own motivation. As mentioned earlier, our differing personalities meant that if Chris had remained as captain in 1985, Stuart Waterton would have been chosen ahead of me as Kent's number one 'keeper.

Chris Cowdrey was the diametric opposite to his predecessor. They had a Christian name in common but that was about it. Cowdrey was all get-up-and-go and for me the perfect captain play to under. His flamboyant, daring style meant that he wouldn't be afraid to risk losing a game in order to win it. Like a latter day cricketing D'Artagnan, he'd sometimes set ludicrous declarations and would often get away with it. He'd live by the sword and die by it, a motto that I would adopt for myself when I eventually took over in the hot seat. On the field, he led from the front. He was an excellent fielder, attacking batsman and, despite being no great shakes as a bowler, had the happy knack of being able to pick up crucial wickets. His infectious enthusiasm rubbed off on the players and he really got us enjoying our cricket.

Chris must have recognised me as kindred spirit as he began to consult me regularly on field placings and bowling changes. Pretty soon it became clear that we had very similar cricketing philosophies and he eventually suggested that I might like to try my hand as vice-captain. Call it lack of ambition, but the idea didn't really appeal to me at the time and I turned him down. I'd always been one of the guys and I thought I'd have to distance myself from players, which is something I didn't want to do. My career was progressing quite nicely and I was enjoying every moment of it. I didn't want to interrupt that by having to change as a person both on and off the field, were I to one day to progress to a higher station.

In 1991, Mark Benson took over the reins and for me his style was an amalgam of Tavaré's and Cowdrey's. He may have given the impression that he was pretty dour, staid and conservative, but in fact he was incredibly shrewd and possessed a fine cricketing brain. He seemed to be able to second-guess the opposing skipper's intentions and would make some very adventurous declarations that to the rest of us appeared to be at least as cranky as Cowdrey's. Whether it was his sharply honed gambler's mind (some of his dubious betting exploits will be chronicled later) I don't know, but as a Benson who definitely knew his hedges, he was extremely canny at processing the odds and playing the percentages.

Although he showed little exuberance on the field and didn't really lead by the swashbuckling example of a Chris Cowdrey, I nevertheless learnt a great deal from Mark. Gradually our rapport developed and, in October 1990, he asked me to become his vice-captain on the basis that being a wicket-keeper, extrovert and a natural motivator, I was in a good position to exert a positive influence on the team without having to compromise my relationship with the rest of the players. Having finally accepted Mark's offer, I summed up my laid-back attitude to the appointment to the *Kent Messenger*: 'In previous years I have always given my point of view because I am probably in the best position to see what was going on. I think I am reasonably good at motivating people and hopefully I will be more so now that I have got a bit more influence. There is so much to think about being captain, I will just be trying to ease the pressure.' Mark was unfortunate with injuries throughout his career and I was soon having to remove my poshest blazer from the wardrobe with increasing regularity. Yet although these matches went quite well, my agenda remained simply to carry out my duties as vice-captain. As usual, I had no higher goal or destiny in mind, I was just going with the flow.

The 1995 Axa, Equity and Law Sunday League title finally saw the Kent trophy drought broken. From the outset, I had known we were in with a realistic chance of improving on our third place of the previous season. The prospect of the guile and improvisation of the diminutive Sri Lankan genius Aravinda de Silva, in tandem with the big-hitting quartet of Trevor Ward, Graham Cowdrey, Matthew Fleming and Mark Ealham, was mouth-watering. The side was jam-packed with all-rounders, we batted down to number ten, and in Macca and Dean Headley, the cream of our bowling attack was test class.

Although it took a great team effort to win thirteen out of sixteen matches, special mention has to made of Graham Cowdrey. When he was in a positive frame of mind there were few more destructive batsmen, and his three early season unbeaten knocks of 92, 105 and 101 against Leicestershire, Hampshire and Middlesex put our marker down for the for the rest of the campaign.

In the Sunday League, you can't allow yourself much more than a single defeat in the first half of the season if you have any aspirations at all of winning the title. It's full-on cricket and the slightest slip can deal your hopes a fatal blow. Having faltered after an all-conquering start, we knew the match against Derbyshire was crucial. Mark Ealham's response couldn't have been more emphatic. Having come in when his side was struggling at 105 for 5, Mark vaporised the Sunday League record for the fastest century by blasting nine fours and nine sixes in his forty ball hundred. He gave three chances but was hitting the ball with such power and ferocity that when he pulled one straight to Chris Adams at square leg, it still rocketed through his hands for six! If Karl Krikken could have followed suit and dumped the last ball of Derbyshire's reply into the crowd, all Mark's heroics would have gone agonisingly to waste. Fortunately they scrambled only two and we held on to win a memorable game by four runs. It was a highly significant match not only from a team perspective, but for me personally. Mark Benson's misfortune in breaking a finger while fielding meant I'd be acting skipper for the Benson & Hedges final the following Saturday.

It took Mark a month or so to recover and I was left holding the baby for the next five matches. Although we were undone by Kevin Curran's maiden Sunday League century in my first game against Northants, we managed to win the remainder, with Aravinda de Silva's and Trevor Ward's monster partnership of 241 versus Surrey, a Kent record for the Sunday League, being the highlight.

For the match against Nottinghamshire at Trent Bridge I joined Mark on the sick list with an injured finger so Aravinda took over as skipper. His "alleged" antics at the toss would reveal one of the first suggestions of the mile-wide streak of cunning that runs through the otherwise unassuming disposition of your average Sri Lankan cricketer. Onlookers from the balcony saw Tim Robinson, the Notts captain, spin the coin and then stand there shaking his head dumbfounded as Aravinda briskly toddled his way back to the pavilion. 'I think I've been done!' gasped Tim to his puzzled team-mates afterwards. Apparently while the coin was in the air, Aravinda mumbled some semi-audible concoction of 'heads' and 'tails', snatched it up almost before it had hit the ground, shook Tim's hand, said 'I think we'll have a bat' and strutted off back to the dressing-room! "Gobsmacked" is one of today's more revolting clichés, but it summed up Tim's expression to a tee. It didn't do us a lot of good though, we lost the match by nine wickets!

In the final match of a very tightly contested season we were assured that victory over our old enemies, Warwickshire, who had beaten us in our last six meetings, would bring the title back to Kent. It would have been doubly satisfying to beat our bogey side in the process but, true to form in recent years, we trod on a banana skin as we dipped for the line. But for once the gods were smiling on us. Although we were beaten by five wickets, Worcestershire, our main rivals, had their game abandoned and finished up sharing top spot with us and Warwickshire. The Carol Vordermans in the side had, however, already totted up that Graham's and Mark's prolific exploits with the bat had blessed us with an unassailable run rate.

In was unfortunate that we'd acquired our first piece of silverware in not much short of a generation thanks to the limpest of technicalities. Nevertheless, the carpers who tried to belittle our achievement by branding it a hollow victory hugely irritated me. The vagaries of the English summer give rise to all sorts of ifs and maybes. While the timing of Worcester's last day washout may have looked cruel, it may have all been academic if our early season clash with a struggling Durham side hadn't also fallen foul of the elements. It's all swings and roundabouts and Kent thoroughly deserved to be Sunday League champions in 1995.

While the immediate aftermath of the game was tinged with anti-climax, it didn't take too long for the post match celebrations to roar into full swing. With four thousand of the Kent faithful partying outside, the dressing-room was euphoric. Dean Headley was wandering around with a cigarette drooping out of his mouth looking like a dusky James Dean and even the opposition skipper, Dermot Reeve, whipped out his guitar and started taking requests! It was quite simply the greatest day of my career. The sweet smell of success was quite intoxicating and I was now craving for more.

I'd gone on record saying several times that once we managed to win one trophy, more would quickly follow. It was sad that the chief architect of our success in '95, Mark Benson, would not be part of it. He aggravated a long-term knee injury in a pre-season kick-about and, although we didn't realise it at the time, he'd already played his last game for Kent. It was fitting that his last act was to accept our first trophy since the shared County Championship in 1978 and I thought it was a superb gesture for him to invite me to come forward and raise it with him.

Following Mark's injury I ended up captaining the side *de facto* for the whole of 1996. In a scenario very similar to that which saw me don the gloves for a the first time at Lordswood, somebody else's unfortunate injury pushed me unexpectedly in a direction I could never have envisaged for myself.

With the players responding well to me - Dean Headley would later say that the 1996 season was the most enjoyable he'd ever played - I gradually started to believe that captaincy might be something I'd enjoy. I felt that as years went on, my England prospects were dwindling, so the only major challenge left for me would be to captain the county and hopefully win trophies.

Three quarters of the way through the summer, Mark announced his retirement and I was formally made captain. It was a superb moment, although the kudos almost seemed to mean more to my parents than it did to me. My mother was so thrilled to see her son's name on the captains' board at Canterbury that she snapped it from about fifteen different angles!

The ironic thing was that my promotion actually made me financially worse off! As vice-captain I used to get an allowance, and every time I was captain, I'd get an extra £40 on top of that. On the basis of one hundred days' cricket per season, it all worked out to a far from paltry £4,000. Sadly, the "all inclusive" package I got as official captain meant that I ended up out of pocket in net terms. Nevertheless I don't think there are many cricketers out there who would begrudge paying a small financial premium for the honour of captaining their county, especially one of the stature of Kent.

The prestige of the captaincy was fantastic but at times I was rather dubious as to whether it quite compensated for the extra hassle I had to put up with. For one thing, it hoovered up so much of my time. Not only was there the never-ending cycle of committee meetings to contend with, but I also had to make myself constantly available for the press. In many ways, the toughest part of the job was dealing with the press, especially after bad results. As a player you can go and hide in a corner and feel sorry for yourself for a while and then slide off unnoticed. As a skipper you have to somehow mask your emotions and then go out and give them what they want. The club doesn't give you any media training - you either sink or swim.

These side issues were not, however, going to distract me from my primary quest and, as we entered the final phase of the 1996 season, the County Championship looked as if it could be swinging our way. While our Sunday League form had nose-dived, some breathtaking individual performances had lifted us from rock bottom of the championship pile in '95 to its summit in '96. With the ball, Dean Headley's hat-tricks in successive matches against Derbyshire and Worcestershire confirmed the maturity of the exceptional talent we all knew he possessed, and with the bat, nothing could eclipse Matthew Walker's record-breaking 275 not out against Somerset at Canterbury.

Going into the penultimate game of the season, we were top of the table by one point, following a seven wicket victory - our eighth of the campaign - over Nottinghamshire at Tunbridge Wells. Against Hampshire at Canterbury it was imperative that we held our nerve against a side languishing deep in the bottom third of the table, and a first innings total of 445, including 130 from Nigel Llong, put us nicely in the driving seat. A battling century by Jason Laney put steel into the visitors' reply - that was until Dean Headley hit back with his third hat-trick of the season (thereby equalling the world record) and reduced them to 358. Hampshire needed 299 to win on the last day and by lunch they were looking favourites on 113 for 1. Perhaps smarting that Deano had stolen his thunder yet again, Martin McCague came out after the interval like a man possessed. On his way to figures of 6 for 51 he rampaged through five Hampshire batmen, including another remarkable hat-trick, and by the time Matthew Fleming had mopped up the tail, the visitors had capitulated to 150 all out.

In our final match against Gloucestershire at Bristol, we knew we had to win and hope that Leicestershire and Surrey slipped up. With the Foxes only needing maximum bonus points to guarantee them the title, we probably already knew that the writing was on the wall and we crumpled to a ten wicket defeat inside three days. As if to twist the knife further, Derbyshire's victory over Durham saw them leap-frog into second place and dump us down to fourth. Over the course of what was in many ways a very memorable season, we'd fought like Greeks only to be cut down at the last. The need to lift the guys after such a bitter finale was to prove the keenest test of my captaincy to date.

As the previous two seasons had amply illustrated, Kent cricket in the nineties was the original curate's egg. We'd be propping up the table one year and then challenging for a title the next. There was no rhyme or reason to it. We had plenty of talent, but no consistency. At the start of '97 I told the side that there was no reason why we couldn't go out and win all four trophies. But we had to believe in ourselves. We had to look like winners and behave like winners. Just as importantly, we needed to play with a certain swagger, a certain arrogance, and if that meant upsetting a few sensibilities, then so much the better. Kent were going to play hard ball.

My determination that 1997 was going to be different was summed up by my pre-season comments to the *Daily Telegraph*: 'In the past there has been a tendency for Kent, particularly after an injury prone start, to claim we're only suited to the one-day game and shrug off the long championship campaign. That attitude's no longer valid. We have experience, a marvellous camaraderie and an intake that will give us a real buzz.'

The new "intake" to which I was referring was the Zimbabwean leg-spinner Paul Strang and the prolific former England batsman Alan Wells. As Carl Hooper's replacement while the Guyanan was touring with the West Indies, Paul was an absolute gem of a signing. A test-class wrist spinner with all the variations, he was a useful lower-order batsman whose fielding, some said, stood comparison with Jonty Rhodes'. His haul of 61 championship wickets in '97 would speak for itself.

Wells' signing was more contentious. Many Kent supporters questioned the wisdom of signing a thirty-five-year-old on a five year contract, especially when his arrival from war-torn Sussex prompted the exit in the opposite direction of crowd favourite Neil Taylor. Over the previous ten to fifteen years Neil, along with Mark Benson, had been perhaps the county's most consistent performer with the bat and was both fearless and combative against all types of bowling. As time went on, however, I felt that he'd become a little bit selfish in his batting. As a batsman matures into his mid-thirties, he starts to look nervously over his shoulder at the younger pretenders and adjusts his way of playing accordingly. I began to sense that Neil was placing too high a priority on the preservation of his average. I remember a match against Lancashire at Lytham when Neil padded back an entire over of spin from Alex Barnett in what looked like an attempt to steer clear of a ferocious Wasim Akram. Something similar arose when Neil was due to go in to face a particularly fiery Curtly Ambrose. All of a sudden he would complain of a migraine, only to appear to make a miraculous recovery a quarter of an hour later when the coast was clear. It surprised me because Neil was a superb player of quick bowling and I could only assume he'd started to doubt his own ability as the first tiny fissures in his steely temperament were beginning to widen.

Bearing in mind our lack of real quality at the top of the order, the availability of Wells, after his well publicised rift with Sussex, became too tempting to resist. It was a gamble, but I felt that with Alan we'd get Neil's runs back and, at the same time, gain ourselves a better team player. To be fair, he played his full part in our success in 1997 and was the only Kent batsman to accumulate over 1,000 first-class runs.

During the winter, our coach Daryl Foster's contract was terminated and we found ourselves under the tutelage of an untried new incumbent, the former New Zealand top-order batsman John Wright. Though I had a great deal of respect for Daryl, John's technical astuteness, tungsten resolve and skilled man-management quickly compensated for his lack of senior coaching experience, and our relationship developed rapidly into one of harmony and mutual respect. 'John thinks about the game the same way I do,' I told the *Daily Express* on the forty-two-year-old's appointment in March, 'he was a gutsy player with a big will to win and I am looking forward to working with him.'

I knew we had to get on a roll early because the only way to generate genuine team spirit is to get some early victories under your belt. Once a side gets into bad run, morale evaporates rapidly. Team underperformance puts players under pressure for their places and they gradually start to begrudge their team-mates' success and even hope they fail. Everyone's prime motivation is self-preservation and the unit splinters into eleven individuals.

So from day one I concentrated on getting the guys relaxed and enthusiastic and encouraged them not to be frightened about playing for one another. The game's packed with egocentrics whose only concern is their own performance and their own careers. Whether the team does well or not is not a factor for them; they're pulling up the ladder at the first opportunity. Yet in 1997 we had a group of guys who were genuinely pleased for each other's success. This started in pre-season when, instead of getting stale through

Graham Gooch-style fitness regimes and morning and afternoon net sessions, we broke up the routine with events like paint-balling or karting. Occasionally, we would spend a day at a hotel doing gym work in the morning and golf in the afternoon. People talk about "team bonding", but I felt the more we got the guys enjoying what they did, the more we would get out of them as players.

I was also a firm believer in getting the maximum from the guys by letting them express their individuality. Yet if they were determined to hang themselves, I'd be there spooling out the hemp. It had to be that way because my own personality dictated that I played hard and socialised hard, so if I was out on the tiles, I could then hardly expect the rest of the team to be in bed by ten with lights out. In other words, if you do want to have a few beers after the game and roll in a three o'clock in the morning, that's fine, as long as you perform the next day. Obviously you can't do that day in, day out. You have to pick your moments and understand your own strengths and weaknesses. But at least everyone in the side felt they were part of it and were there because they could express their natural ability. Too many coaches and captains put too much pressure on individuals and in doing so inhibit their talent.

Team meetings were always very inclusive affairs and I tried to involve as many people as possible in the making of decisions. From the most senior professional to the rawest of new recruits, everyone's opinion was valuable. By validating each person's input, no player could feel that he was being excluded and this was vital in bonding the team together. 'If you run a dictatorship,' I told the *Kent Messenger*, 'then people don't feel part of it, they're just led along. My philosophy is to give everyone a view. They are professionals; quality players and I like to keep an open dialogue.' It turned out to be a cornerstone in my strategy to gel the squad into a robust, contented unit and was a major contributory factor in the success we enjoyed in the annus *semi*-mirabilis, 1997. You could sense the bubble of enthusiasm that was building within the squad and the positiveness of their attitude was evident right from the first game. 1997 turned out to be a very good year, but it came within a tantalising whisker of being an absolutely unbelievable one. We got onto that winning roll early and the bandwagon appeared to be gathering what we hoped was an unstoppable momentum. Although our performance in the final of the Benson & Hedges Cup had been a bitter disappointment, we were still set fair in both the Sunday League and the County Championship as the season drew towards its climax. An unlikely four run victory over Middlesex at Lord's (a mere two weeks after our humbling in the B&H) looked to have set up our dash for the championship crown and, after an innings win over Essex, we travelled down to Taunton for our fourth-to-last game of the season. Little things, alas, can mean the difference between hell and glory. Paul Strang's 6 for 72 meant that we required 161 to win the match on the final day, an equation that was eventually whittled down to seven runs needed off the final over. If there was one individual at the club you would hand pick to be taking strike at the beginning of that fateful over it would be Matthew Fleming. With England one-day international appearances under his belt and a reputation as the county's fiercest striker of a cricket ball, it seemed completely unfeasible that we wouldn't make it home.

If Joel Garner, in his pomp, had still been turning his arm over for Somerset, it would have been more understandable and far less traumatic. However, by the time I had come to the crease to face the last ball, Jazzer and Paul Strang had only managed to eke out four singles off the wholly unintimidating Michael Burns. Needing three to win, I scrambled two to level up the scores. It was a slip that would cost us dear in the final analysis.

After thumping Gloucestershire by 274 runs, it was our failure to beat Yorkshire at Headingley (something we hadn't managed in the championship since the war) that sealed our fate. In reply to Yorkshire's first innings total of 312, we were struggling at 202 for 7 when Jazzer and I put up a vigorous rearguard action to give us a decent lead of 62 and full batting points. Chasing 240 to win at less than three an over wasn't a big ask, but Chris Silverwood had different ideas. His inspired 5 for 55 (after 7 for 93 in the first innings) reduced us to 48 for 5 until Jazzer once again came to the rescue, this time aided by Mark Ealham. The draw still kept us in the hunt but, crucially, we'd slipped one point behind Glamorgan and our destiny was now out of our hands.

In the final game against Surrey, any hopes of clawing back the deficit were almost immediately scuppered by an evil Canterbury wicket. On a pitch subsequently rated "poor" by the ECB track police, 19 wickets fell on the first day for a paltry 241 runs. Out of the window flew three precious batting points, closely followed by any real aspirations of the title. David Fulton's maiden championship century won us the game but, in the end, it was all academic as Glamorgan took maximum points at Taunton to finish four clear. 'We may be the bridesmaids,' commented Matthew Fleming, 'but at least we're getting to the wedding.' It just about summed up our summer as cricket's nearly-men. We weren't even catching the bouquet.

The third leg of the triple whammy from hell had occurred the previous weekend when our dismal display at Leeds allowed second-placed Warwickshire to snatch the Sunday League title from under our noses at the last gasp. No wonder people were starting to call us chokers.

An hour after the match I faced the press and television to regurgitate the same old spiel that yes, we'd blown it again despite getting so close and no, we didn't know why. We ended up going to the pub at the end of the road at Headingley as we were staying up to finish the championship match the following day. I was with a few team-mates and my family when I was button-holed by one of the supporters. This guy had obviously had one over the eight, and I suppose you had to forgive him for that, but he then started the "do you know how far we've come to support you and you bottlers let us down continuously" routine.

I had to speak to his friend behind, who was slightly more coherent, and told him to relay the message that there was no one more disappointed than me and the team and that the mood in the dressing-room after the game was almost post-apocalyptic. This guy would nevertheless not let it go, and you get to a point where you've had it for an hour and you feel yourself starting to reach the end of your tether. In the end I had to get one of the players to tell this bloke to basically fox-trot oscar as he was getting himself in pole position for a slap. The boundaries of my composure would never again be so sorely tested.

At the time I went to the press and said yes, maybe we were bottlers. We'd get to the big games and we'd choke for no apparent reason. In reality, we actually did damn well to get as far as we did. For virtually the whole summer we'd been forced to play catch-up cricket as time and time again the top order batting had failed to do its job. By the July of '97 the *Daily Telegraph* had spotted the flaw in our make-up: 'The suspicion that Kent have developed an uncanny talent for extracting themselves from sizeable holes this season is borne out by the figures. In the last 14 championship innings in which they have lost nine or all 10 wickets, the second five have outscored the first five on nine occasions.' It was a fair point. I was a regular number eight batsman in '97 and ended up finishing second in the averages. We were winning games by the seat of our pants, with our fighting spirit alone seeing us through at the critical moment. We'd been punching well above our weight in '97 and, to put it bluntly, we didn't have the class to sustain the pace. At some stage or another, our luck was bound to run out.

Despite finishing up empty handed, there was still much to be taken from the 1997 season. We'd shown a far greater depth of character in our three-pronged title chase and proved ourselves to be one of the top two or three teams in the country. My marshalling of the guys had won some favourable reviews and there was no more meaningful endorsement than that paid to me by Lord Cowdrey: 'As a former captain I would especially congratulate Steve for his captaincy, and his stamina in keeping wicket well and producing some fine innings...it was one of the most memorable seasons in the history of the club.' That was good enough for me.

From the outset as captain, I'd always assured the players that they could be completely up front with me with any grievance they had and, in turn, I would be totally open with them. At the start of a season, a lot of teams used to pay lip service to "honesty", but I meant what I said, one hundred per cent. For the team to function properly as a unit, I couldn't afford to let any niggles, however minor, fester into open sores. I therefore actively encouraged players to come to me with any gripe and I'd do my best to explain my line of thinking as clearly and fairly as possible. I didn't care what vitriol they threw at me, as long as they didn't go behind my back. This policy of total candour made some difficult decisions even harder, especially when it involved players I regarded as close friends.

So the decision to drop my longest-standing pal and comedy side-kick, Graham Cowdrey, was one of the most difficult I ever had to make. Just over half-way through the season we were about to go to Derby in the championship and we were just starting to go off the boil. You couldn't single anybody out, but we just seemed to be struggling at the top of the order, so I said to John Wright that I thought we needed a change. Nobody was doing brilliantly, nobody was doing badly, we just appeared to be over-endowed with batsmen averaging a mediocre twenty-odd.

As there was no obvious candidate for the chop, we decided to base our decision on performances over the last four games. As it happened, Graham's average was slightly worse than the others. The easier option would have been for me to fob off one of the younger guys with the patronising offer of a "rest", but it wasn't something I was prepared to do. Such a cop-out meant that I wouldn't have been true to my word at the start of the season, so I bit the bullet and went to Graham to tell him he wasn't going to Derbyshire. He naturally asked why, so I gave him the reasons and asked that he took it as a man and a friend. Regrettably he reacted by telling me that we wouldn't win another game that season by dropping him. In the end, rain interrupted the game at Derby, although had it not, we would have enjoyed a comfortable win. But overall, I believe my decision was seen to be correct as our season began to take off again.

Established batsmen now realised that their comfort zone no longer existed and that they were liable to be dropped as soon as their performances failed to come up to scratch. It certainly focused a few people's minds.

Sometimes you had to give the team a collective kick up the backside and take a calculated gamble to draft in a second-teamer. To be fair it tarnished mine and Graham's friendship for a little while. We weren't quite as close as we were for a time, but fortunately we're now good mates again. I fully understood his disappointment at the way it was done, but when you're coming down to the wire in three title chases, sometimes old friendships and loyalties have to be put to one side.

Probably my best pal in the side was that Anglo-Aussie Ulsterman, Martin McCague. But you wouldn't have guessed it after some of the stand up rows we used to have on the cricket field. I felt I knew how to get this talented and aggressive fast-bowler firing, and if I sensed he was unconsciously just going through the motions, I'd sometimes take him off after two overs. Once the standard reply of 'What the fuck are you doing?' wafted back in my direction, it all usually prompted a forthright and highly agricultural exchange of views. It's the most basic of psychological ploys, but nine times out of ten it worked a treat as he'd come back tearing off batmen's heads again trying to stick it back up me.

Basically Macca and I could always say what we liked to each other because we knew we were good mates and it would all be forgotten again in a couple or so overs. I couldn't however afford to be so robust with all the members of the strike force. I rated Mark Ealham probably my most reliable and consistent performer with the ball whose accurate swing bowling got us out of many a tight situation. Nevertheless, you had to be careful not to steam in too hard if he'd lost his rhythm as he'd be just as likely to tell you "bollocks" and not try at all. Another candidate for the softly-softly approach was Dean Headley. Deano would have a different theory for every ball he bowled and at the very least you had to pretend you had an inkling of what he was trying to achieve. 'Yes, that's very good Dean,' I'd cajole, 'how about bowling it just a *little* bit faster next time?' He was also the nicest fast bowler in the history of the game. If a batsman said "good ball" to one of his bouncers, he turn round and smile at him. If he'd had a bit more of the Aussie mentality and stared, growled and cussed, I'm sure his collection of England caps would have come close to matching the much higher number that his huge talent deserved.

The one player I could never get through to was the West Indian Carl Hooper. He had all the talent in the world but sadly none of the application. That's not to say I didn't like Carl, because I did, but at times he was so diffident and disinterested, it was a wonder he managed to stay awake. I remember once at Canterbury he was perched on the balcony engaged in a marathon mobile phone conversation with his girlfriend. He was on it right the way through the morning session, charged it up again over lunch, and was then on it again for the entire afternoon session. The incredible part was that his girlfriend was living in Australia at the time and the call cost him about £300! In the end you'd virtually have to kick the chair away from under him to get him to go out to bat!

Typical of his attitude was his famous no-show at the start of the 1998 season. He'd already been giving the West Indies the runaround with his antics, complaining of personal problems and some mystery virus, and now it was our turn.

With nobody having seen hide nor hair of him on the morning of the first championship game, John Wright and I went round to his digs to see what the situation was. He was indeed at home and I advised him that we had a game starting in two hours and that, as we'd contracted him to play cricket, it would be awfully nice of him if he could perhaps collect his kit together and make his way to the ground. To my astonishment, he replied that he wasn't going to play because he had too much to sort out with the house!

There was no point whatsoever in forcing him to do anything because he just wouldn't respond. The problem was that after Paul Strang's excellent contribution as our overseas player in the previous season, Carl's "unhelpful" attitude started rocking the boat from day one. My carefully fostered spirit of team unity was being undermined by this temperamental maverick who gave the impression that his only motivation was financial. Carl obviously regarded himself as a special case and was constantly turning up late and missing net sessions.

Concerned about the negative influence this was undoubtedly having on the team, I got the rest of the guys together and said that we could play the Hooper situation one of two ways. I could either tell him that he's to turn up to every training session punctually or he'll get fined until he squeaked, or we'd write him off as a part of our unit and let him do his own thing. The first option guaranteed that he would always turn up on time because he wouldn't want to be hit in the back pocket, but it also meant that he was likely to sulk for the rest of the season and give us zilch in terms of performances. In the end the guys unanimously went for the second option, as that would at least mean that we would get the occasional big knock from him. It was a great pity because having such a key player as an outsider took the edge off our spirit and no doubt contributed in some way to a disappointing 1998 season.

Of course having decided to stay on the outside, Carl couldn't have his cake and eat it. He'd set himself apart from the rest of us and that's where he'd have to stay. In one of our team meetings he had the nerve to pipe up and complain that the side was soft and lacking in the desire and belief to win. That was a red rag to Graham Cowdrey and he launched into him.

'Hang on a second Carl, you are actually talking about yourself! How many games have you actually won for us? Okay, you score runs but there has only been one game in which you've played a knock that really mattered.'

And he was quite right. Carl would score well in the first innings, or in the second innings when we were trying to save the game, but in one-day matches when the chips were down, he'd be back in the pavilion before you could say "rum make ya happy?"

The extent to which Carl would keep himself to himself was highlighted by his refusal to take a shower with the rest of us after the game. Yes, I can safely say that the contents of Carl Hooper's lunch box remained a mystery to all of us. It all led us to surmise that, although he was a West Indian, he was very much an Englishman in that crucial department.

As a captain, my focus was always directed at getting the maximum from my own players rather than worrying too much about the opposition. You'd pick out maybe a few key points of their top players, but generally even then you know where their strengths are going to be - top players tend not to have too many weaknesses. Instead of spending hours analysing videos or scribbling out convoluted game plans, I'd tell the guys to give the opposition respect, but only a little. If we stick to worrying about our own performance and strive to play to the best of our abilities, then the result is irrelevant. If you perform to the maximum of your potential, you'll win the game nine times out of ten. If you lose having performed to your maximum potential, then the opposition is better than you. It's as simple as that. This is not to say the we let the opposition off scot-free. When players came out to bat against us we decided to turn the middle into a lion's den. There didn't have to be too much verbal - it was a case of creating an atmosphere of hostility through aggressive body language. If you can keep it up, there's not too many guys around who can take that kind of psychological battering for too long. You wouldn't, for instance, see any of my players clap an opposition fifty. It was alright to pat them on the back afterwards in the bar, but out in the middle even the insincerest of two-finger ripples would be greeted by a death stare from the skipper. A belligerence of posture wasn't enough on its own as you had to back it up with disciplined bowling and efficiency in the field.

So in order to maintain the guys' focus, I'd encourage them to mentally break down the game into units, whether it be an over, an hour or a session. If we succeeded in winning more units than the opposition then we would win the game.

In terms of strategy, I took a leaf out of Mark Benson's book and played the percentage game. I worked on the "nothing ventured, nothing gained" principle and was prepared to take a few calculated risks. In one-day cricket for example, I'd rather have lost a game with fifteen overs to go by being too bold, than lose four on the trot in the last over by being too conservative. By forcing the opposition go out and win the game, you have more chance of winning it yourself. For example, if your opponents were on top, rather than move the field back and let them stroll to victory, I'd bring the field right in for part, or all of an over just to get them thinking. The idea was to pressurise them into hitting over the top and thereby forcing them to take the initiative. There aren't that many quality outfits on the scene that can pick up that sort of gauntlet, day in, day out, and as a strategy I think my record shows it was pretty successful.

On a personal level, my cricket was actually thriving on the extra responsibilities and pressures of the captaincy. 'According to the sages,' wrote Alexander Clyde in the *Evening Standard*, 'it is virtually impossible to direct operations from behind the stumps, keep up a dialogue with your bowler and maintain the high level of concentration necessary to be a top 'keeper. One man who is currently combining the two jobs with conspicuous success, and keeping a smile on his face, is Kent captain Steve Marsh.' In the early days I have to admit I found it mentally very draining but after a while I managed to find a happy medium whereby I could switch my concentration between wicket-keeping and tactics. It was satisfying and surprising that I could juggle both roles so effectively. I was named Kent's player of the season in 1997 having enjoyed my third best year with the gloves (63 first-class dismissals) and my best season with the bat (first-class average of 39.85).

There can surely be no other sport where the captain plays such a pivotal role in the management of a game. He's in charge of the team selection, strategy, tactics, motivation, discipline and also has to lead by example through his on-field performances. It also helps to be a diplomat. The first championship game in 1997 was held up for half an hour when it was spotted that Derbyshire's left armer, Kevin Dean, who'd come on to bowl the sixth over, was not on their skipper Dean Jones', team sheet. I had to go out into the middle with secretary Stuart Anderson and after a five minute discussion with the umpires, Peter Willey and Ken Palmer, we accepted the mistake had been genuine and that the game could continue.

What many people also forget is the horse-trading that goes on between captains back in the pavilion in order to force a result in matches that look doomed to peter out as draws. If you've got a little of the Henry Kissingers about you, you can often negotiate yourself out of a frustrating stalemate to set up an unlikely victory. Three-day cricket was notorious for causing ridiculously contrived finishes, and more often than not the better side lost. To engineer a decent game of cricket you had to know how to do it, especially as improving wickets meant that declaration bargaining was starting to creep into the four-day version as well. It was like bartering in a Moroccan bazaar. If you needed a result on the last day you'd go to the opposition skipper and if they were batting last you kept offering them revised targets until they decided to play ball. Not all captains stuck to the rules, however. When we were playing a championship game against Glamorgan at Cardiff in 1996, I agreed with their captain, Matthew Maynard, that we would make a game of it and I would set them a reachable target to chase batting last. Then the rains came and we had to renegotiate. He wasn't keen at first, but we finally agreed after I'd offered him twenty free runs under the proviso that, whatever happened, they went all the way. They stayed level with the asking rate initially, then lost a couple of quick wickets. We then gave them some more runs and then they lost a couple more. We'd got them six down when their West Indian overseas player, Ottis Gibson, who had just been given the sack, mysteriously decided to turn very un-Caribbean and dead-bat everything. After traipsing in without having shaken hands after the inevitable draw, I tackled Matthew who tried to convince me that Gibson had taken it upon himself to shut up shop. I found that hard to believe, because if I'd just been sacked, the last thing I'd be doing would be digging in to help the side save a game.

As a skipper, my word was my bond and I always stuck to my side of the bargain. You could only ever stitch somebody up once and suddenly you'll find yourself with an unwelcome reputation in the relatively small church that is county cricket.

When you appreciate how much negotiation and bargaining actually goes on to somehow contrive a result, it's little wonder that the game has eventually been tainted with match fixing allegations. Because captains have so much influence on how the game functions they can occasionally become prey to the unscrupulous. One unguarded comment can lead to all sorts of misinterpretation and all of a sudden a captain is left with an indelibly blemished reputation. That said, I have never known of any betting coups in the county game, let alone been involved in one myself. Admittedly it was occasionally a topic of conversation in the Kent dressing-room. There would be the likes of myself, Graham Cowdrey, Mark Benson and a few others looking at Gloucestershire at 7/4 to beat Kent in a meaningless mid-table Sunday League game and thinking how nice it would be to whip round to Ladbrokes with the contents of our respective piggy banks. But that's as far as it got, honest guv!

Along with a few others I always knew that Matthew Fleming was born to captain Kent. Whether he had a right to do so was highly debatable but nevertheless that was the view of a sizeable segment of the committee, including the highly influential Jim Swanton and a significant number of county members. I think it hurt the Fleming camp that we did so well in 1997 as I believe that they had pencilled in 1998 as the year to trump up an excuse and oust me from the captaincy. They knew they didn't have a lot of time as their man was pushing his mid-thirties and getting very close to his sell-by date as a player. Soon it would be too late for him.

From the off it was obvious that Jazzer and I weren't exactly hewn from the same stone. He'd been to Eton, came from one of the richest families on the planet and was an officer and a gentleman who'd served Queen and country in the Royal Green Jackets. In contrast I'd never set foot in a public school, wore a dodgy mullet, spoke with a Medway accent and had the reputation of being a bit of a happy-go-lucky lad-about-town. So for the old school tie brigade who preferred a "good old-fashioned game of cricket, one off the mark and jolly good show", my in-your-face style of captaincy was far removed from the perceived Kent ethos. It didn't matter if we won nothing as long as everyone thought we were "bloody nice blokes".

In September 1994, after my first few games deputising for Mark Benson, a wise sage at *The Observer* foresaw the discomfort that my appointment would provoke in some quarters: 'In his place, Marsh has led the team with distinction, and in time he is the obvious choice to succeed Benson as club captain, though there are still those on the Kent committee who pine for a more blue-blooded leader.' Prophetic indeed.

So although it grated on them that we did so well in '97, they were bound to keep me on as captain in 1998 and hope that something would then go wrong. Admittedly, by comparison with the previous year, '98 was a slight disappointment as, although we finished fourth in the Sunday League and made the quarter-finals in one of the cups, we could only finish eleventh in the County Championship. I'm not one to bear grudges, but what deeply disappointed me during that season was that I knew Jazzer had been lobbying to take over as captain. I could sense that he was trying to force the issue when on one or two occasions he would instigate a team meeting as he felt we weren't doing well enough and something had to be done. Gradually a rift began to appear in my carefully constructed unit and I believe that Jazzer was the chief culprit.

At the end of the season I knew that there had been some rumblings. I'd heard that concerns had been raised about some players' off-field activities, even though late nights had never been an issue when we'd been doing so well the previous season. I therefore decided to call a team meeting after a training session at Canterbury in an attempt to clear the air.

'Enough's enough,' I said, 'we've got to get this out in the open. There's seventeen of you here onto one. You've now got the opportunity to get it all off your chests and to shoot me down in flames. I promise I won't take it to heart, but afterwards I can assure you I'll be having my say.' The ensuing cacophony of embarrassed feet shuffling confirmed to me that the one or two who had been stirring the pot had been well towards the back of the queue when moral fibre was being handed out. It never got off the ground.

The writing was nevertheless on the wall and shortly afterwards I was called to the Great Danes Hotel near Maidstone for a showdown with John Wright and Chairman of Cricket, Derek Ufton. After a twenty minute trip round the houses, I put an end to the small talk and cut to the quick.

'OK, what are we doing here?' I ventured, dosing my question with a large slug of mock ignorance.

Derek took a deep breath, repositioned his no doubt uncomfortably sweaty buttocks and replied:

'Well there are some rumblings that the club might want a change of captain.'

Somehow I managed to retain my composure.

'Come on, let's talk straight now, you're talking to me, you *can* be honest. There's not just rumblings, there *is* going to be a change isn't there?'

Derek, who was far too pleasant a guy for his own good,

admitted there was indeed going to be a change. Knowing all along that this was what they had in mind, I went on the front foot.

'Fine, I haven't got a problem with being sacked as long as you can give me reasons why. If you can tell me that the guys have lost respect for me, if you can tell me that I've made some horrendous tactical errors and that my heart's not in it any more, I won't necessarily agree with you, but I'll understand.'

Knowing he was on ground of superlative dodginess, Derek refused to go into specifics, citing his only logic as 'sometimes it's nice to have a change'. If it wasn't so pathetic, I probably would have burst out laughing, but at least it backed up my earlier thought that either Jazzer or his supporters were behind it all. Without them fanning the flames, I am positive I would have been retained as captain for 1999.

I wasn't going to let either of them off the hook and, as the meeting went on, Derek started to dig himself an even larger hole. He then came out with one of the most ludicrous statements I'd ever heard pass the lips of a cricket administrator. He said he thought a change of captain might mean a change of luck, and when I challenged him on what sort of "luck" he had in mind, he suggested that there had been a few important tosses that I'd lost. He probably regretted coming out with such a crass comment and after I picked my jaw up from the floor I pointed out that if that's what decides a captain then what chance have I got? I didn't realise I was that much of a useless tosser.

Derek pretty much conceded the argument to me when he admitted 'You're actually putting up a better case for keeping the job than we are for changing it'. I knew full well, however, that I was looking at the wrong end of a done-deal, but I was still determined to have my say.

'Is it the case,' I suggested, 'that the captain and the coach work very closely, hand-in-hand, sharing the decisions on training, tactics and team selection?'

Derek confirmed that to be so and I turned to John Wright, who nodded his agreement. Having directed them neatly down a cul-de-sac, I fixed Derek in my gaze and said, 'OK, if that's the case, then why isn't this man being sacked with me?'

It was a question that, of course, they couldn't answer. Come in number seven, your time is up.

The irony was that off the field John Wright was a really terrific guy who you could have a drink with and easily relate to. But at the committee meeting that was called to decide my fate, he was apparently one of the main trumpeters of the Fleming cause. I believe he felt at the time that he would be able to manipulate Jazzer more when it came to crunch decisions. Although Wright and I hardly ever fell out, I'd always be strong enough to stick to my guns if I felt a decision was right. It was telling that in the 2000 season he admitted to me that he regretted having backed Jazzer over me because he felt our working relationship had been by far the stronger.

The whole affair both disappointed and angered me to such an degree that I felt I couldn't continue playing for Kent and I had a chat with Mike Gatting about moving to Middlesex. The injustice of it all was too much for my father-in-law Bob Wilson and he immediately tendered his resignation from the committee. 'I was very angry at the time and still am,' he hissed, 'I feel Kent have made a scapegoat out of Steve and I don't really want to be associated with those sorts of decisions.' But when the heat had gone out of the situation a few weeks later I reasoned it was something that I had no control over. You can't, after all, dictate where you were born and brought up, and the whole county knew I had nothing whatsoever to reproach myself over. The fact that the committee sent me on my way without even having the decency to tell me why spoke volumes about their real motivation. 'The truth is,' wrote Mark Pennell in the *Kent Messenger*, 'Marsh has been made to pay for the under-achievement of fellow senior players at the club. It is they, as well as the committee, who should be hanging their heads in shame following this latest public relations disaster at the club.'

My determination not to be beaten by these limp personalities made me stay with the county and attempt to put the sorry episode behind me. In the remainder of my career at Canterbury I could have easily been bloody-minded enough to take my foot right off the pedal and throw in some sub-standard displays. However I resolved to give Matthew Fleming my total commitment as a player. If I'd underperformed deliberately I would not have been true to myself and would have gone on to regret it in later life. I accepted the extension to my contract and promised the players they could still rely on me, one hundred per cent. The *Kent Messenger*, in its 1999 end of term report, duly noted that my resolution hadn't flagged: 'After the shoddy way the club handled the end of Marsh's term of captaincy, few would have blamed him for coasting. But he always stood up to be counted and can be well pleased with his overall contributions.'

If the decision to appoint Jazzer was made for purely cricketing reasons, then it has so far failed. Kent continue to underachieve. Most of the current squad will tell you that he has many failings as a captain, although his personal performances with bat and ball have held up well. But barely six weeks into his tenure as skipper, the *Kent Messenger* was already sounding warning bells. Under the headline 'Lack of team spirit is a major problem', it commented, '...even Fleming must realise that you cannot run a cricket side like the Royal Green Jackets. Perhaps a rethink on the man-management front is called for.'

What also amazed me was that his new-found discipline as a batsman had been mysteriously lacking when he played for other captains. It always used to be gung-ho Fleming, batting as if it he'd got Darth Vader's light sabre in his hand. But when he became captain, he'd get stuck in like never before. Read into that what you will.

I took the job of Kent captain for two reasons. Firstly, because it was a privilege and secondly because I sincerely believed I could make that extra difference and turn Kent into a side capable of winning trophies. The core value of my captaincy would be honesty. If I was able to establish a two-way relationship of trust and respect with my players, then I'd have half the battle won. While I may have succeeded in that respect, what I didn't fully appreciate was the requirement to be lucky.

I look back on my two and a half years a Kent captain with a lot of pride. The proportion of matches won under my captaincy actually makes me, in statistical terms, one of the most successful captains in the county's history. In my time at the helm I very quickly learned a great deal about both myself and other people. For one thing, captaincy brought out a natural aptitude for leadership and man-management that I had no idea I possessed. Despite the backstairs intrigues that were plotting my downfall at the end of 1998, the esteem in which the players held me and their encouragement for me to continue leading them was something I'll always cherish.

My pledge of honesty was also my downfall. The county hierarchy, snugly ensconced in its ivory tower, felt uncomfortable that this brash, progressive new captain from the other side of the tracks dared to have a mind of his own. Anybody with a fresh approach that jeopardised the status quo was a threat that had to be eliminated. When my luck ran out, they had their excuse. The committee can console themselves that they've employed one of their own in Matthew Fleming, but when are they finally going to wake up to the real world?

FOUR

Match of my life

There's little that most athletes wouldn't sacrifice in order to leave their indelible mark in the annals of their chosen sport. The fortunate thing for a cricketer is that there is a myriad of opportunities for him to do so. Indeed, there can be surely no other pastime that offers the participant so many spurious chances to be a record holder. In football, you have to be satisfied with accumulating more international caps than Peter Shilton or scoring more goals than Bobby Charlton. If you're a golfer it's only really a case of shooting under sixty or trying to overhaul Jack Nicklaus' gargantuan collection of eighteen majors. However if you happen to wallow in the statistical porridge that is cricket, you could wrest immortality from any one of the umpteen methods listed on the six hundred and ninety pages that make up the *Wisden Book of Cricket Records*.

The nice thing is that you don't have to be particularly any good to earn your entry. V. R. Hogg's beer-tent filling innings of 0 in 87 minutes in Pietermaritzburg in 1979/80 has no less entitlement to a mention than the 101 in forty minutes by G. L. Jessop at Harrogate in 1897. Worcestershire's R. D. Burrows's feat of knocking a bail 67 yards in bowling W. Huddleston of Lancashire in 1911 may well be quirky, but it can nonetheless stand proudly alongside A. F. Kippax's and J. E. H. Hooker's epic tenth wicket stand of 307 for New South Wales against Victoria in 1928/29.

That 307 was an unholy amount of runs for a final pair to amass, but in 1997 at Horsham, Ben Phillips and I managed to spank Sussex for 183 - the sixth highest tenth wicket stand in County Championship history. David Llewellwyn of *The Independent* wasn't far wide of the mark when he wrote 'Not even Mystic Meg could have predicted the goings on here yesterday'. Sussex looked as if they were heading for a win, having reduced us to 257 for 9 at lunch on the third day, a lead of only 238. I'd just put on 60 with Paul Strang for the ninth wicket when Phillips, in only his fourth first-class match, came out to join me. Ben batted beautifully throughout his unbeaten 62 and it wasn't long before the Sussex bowlers and fielders were chasing shadows and booting advertising hoardings in frustration. The only chance I gave in my career best 142 was when Vasbert Drakes kindly carried one of my clouts over the boundary for six! Eventually, after a last wicket joy-ride lasting three and a quarter hours, I skied one to Toby Radford at midwicket and Ben and I left the field leaving Sussex needing a whopping 422. The wicket was benign and it looked like they were guiding themselves to a commendable draw when Macca, having downed his tea-time Shredded Wheat, ripped out six wickets in the final session to win us the game by 104 runs. It was a good one to win and it made me the first wicket-keeper to win the *Evening Standard* Player of the Month award! Woof!

But my real fifteen minutes of fame had come on 1st June 1991 when I equalled the record for dismissals in an innings by taking eight catches against Middlesex at Lord's. In doing so I joined Queenslander Wally Grout, who snapped up his haul of Western Australians at Brisbane in 1959/60, and Essex's David East, who caught the first eight Somerset batsmen on his twenty-sixth birthday in 1985. As a David from Essex, it was obviously a case of "hold me close, don't let me go" on that particular day!

The Kent record of six was achieved an astonishing seven times by Alan Knott and twice by Les Ames, back in the twenties. Away from the stumps, Alan Ealham, probably the best outfielder the county has ever produced, caught five right-handed Gloucestershire batsmen at long-off off Derek Underwood at Folkestone in 1966. Not exactly a combination you really wanted to keep chancing your arm against.

It started off like any other normal game. Middlesex's decision to put us in on winning the toss looked fairly justified as we racked up a meagre first innings total of 160. Although it was a seamer-friendly wicket, we knew we should have made a far better fist of it and would now need to make early inroads into the Middlesex top order to keep ourselves in the game. Fortunately our four-man seam attack of Richard Ellison, Tony Merrick, Chris Penn and Macca got into their stride very quickly and it wasn't long before I'd claimed my first three victims. It was by no means out of the ordinary for a 'keeper to take the first three or four wickets in an innings, so at that stage I wasn't thinking in terms of any *Boys' Own* heroics and open-topped bus parades up Chatham High Street. It was only at the end of the day's play when I had taken six catches with still three wickets to fall that I began to think that a little piece of history could be in the making. I knew I had already equalled the Kent record and a few people were knocking the dust off some old *Wisdens* to try and find out what the world record for the most number of catches actually was. In the end they needn't have bothered as once back in the dressing-room, the newspapers, who never miss a trick, had been hot on the 'phone advising me of the situation and wanting interviews. To be honest, I was chuffed enough as it was. To equal the county record was an achievement to savour, especially when you consider the calibre and reputation of my predecessors.

Although the spotlight had started to shine on me, I wasn't hyped up in any way due to the relative modesty of my feat. In terms of a celebration I ended up going out for nothing more than my regulation pint or two in London with Macca and our old team-mate Danny Kelleher, who had come down for a visit. It actually turned out to be an entertaining evening as, inevitably, we made the pilgrimage from West Hampstead to Stringfellows. As always happens, a couple turns into three or four, which turns into five or six, and by then you're past caring! I'm not sure what time we made it back to the hotel, but I'm sure it was well within the usual curfew of "half past".

The next morning we went out and, tantalisingly, I took the first two catches of the day to equal the record. There was one more wicket to fall, and if I took it, I'd have the record outright. The tension was really starting to build, especially as the final pair, Simon Hughes and Keith Brown, were doing their level best to string out the drama by hanging around far longer than was necessary! While they were obdurately dead-batting and occasionally swishing, all sorts of plots were being hatched to engineer me the final ninth catch. Chris Cowdrey was at slip and said that if it was edged to him, he'd somehow bobble it up for me to grab!

In the end it was a magnificent bit of work by Matthew Fleming that did the trick. Having come on as a substitute fielder, he took a spectacular one-handed slip catch to dismiss Simon Hughes off Richard "Chernobyl" Davis ("Chernobyl" because of his reputation for being a bad reactor at short leg). 'To be honest, we were glad to be off the field,' I told the *Evening Post*, 'It had taken us an hour and forty minutes to get the last three wickets, so I didn't really care how he was out.'

Back in the pavilion, my attitude to the media was pretty blasé. After all, I'd only done what was expected of me. The bowlers had to take a large slice of the credit and my accomplishment had been merely to be in the right place at the right time. Six out of the eight catches were regulation takes off very thin edges that any half-decent club keeper would have bagged. That said, there is no such thing as an undroppable catch. I remember once putting down an absolute sitter attempting to dismiss Graham Gooch off Hartley Alleyne at Chelmsford. He was on seven at the time but then went on to blast a double ton!

That's not to say that there was no merit whatsoever in the achievement. The odds on a keeper being lucky enough to be gifted eight dollies are astronomical - something that is underlined by the fact that it's only been done a handful of times in the long history of first-class cricket. So, in reality, my place in the record books probably owes itself to the first dismissal, a good diving catch to my right to remove Mike Roseberry, and the tricky leg-side dismissal of Neil Williams off Richard Ellison.

In the dressing-room the 'phone was ringing off the wall with the media clamouring for my reaction. Andy Warhol was spot on as after a quarter of an hour of trying to avoid regurgitating every cliché in the book, it was time for us to go out and start our second innings. I was now looking forward to taking stock of my achievement on the balcony, but as so often with Kent over the last nineteen years, the top order filed out and then back again with alarming regularity. It was usually the case that if Mark Benson or Neil Taylor didn't weigh in with something significant, then as a team we tended to struggle. So having dismissed Middlesex for 163, our reply of 137 for 5 was hardly setting the basis for a match-winning lead and my rest didn't last too long.

Still on cloud nine thanks to my new status as a darling of the media - the *News of the World* would blare in banner headlines 'Marsh a Marvel! Kent keeper Steve joins the gr-eights' - I wafted out to the middle very pleased with myself indeed. But after ten minutes or so of circumspect defence I got a very rude wake-up call from Angus Fraser who, not having read the script, got one to seam and bounce and hit me painfully in the ribs. At the time it was the best thing that could have happened as in knocking the wind right out of my sails, it re-focused my mind, and by the end of the day I had progressed to 57.

We then had a break as it was then still the case that a Sunday League game could be crazily sandwiched in the middle of a championship match. So coming back on the Monday I was happy that I'd done my bit and would have settled for just a few more. As it happened I was spurred on by Macca who, in his debut first team game for the county, was naturally eager to make an impression. Eventually, just before lunch I tickled Chas Taylor for a single and came through for my fourth first-class century after two hours and 244 balls. Considering that we're now such good mates, the fact that Macca hung around to see me through to three figures, made the catches record all the more sweet. For me, a record catches haul followed in quick order by a Lord's century turned my achievement into something unique and extra special. 'If I don't ever get the chance to play for England,' I told the *Evening Post*, 'then it is something I can always look back on, beating the greats like Alan Knott, Godfrey Evans and Les Ames. It doesn't mean that I'm as good or better or worse than them, it's just a nice record to have.'

My 66 catches and four stumpings placed me second in the wicket-keepers' table in the 1991 season. At the age of thirty I was moving into my prime as a 'keeper and I hoped that this one game was at last going to give me the recognition and exposure that my overall performances had deserved. I always feared in the back of my mind that there was a perception of "unprofessionalism" in the way I conducted myself off the field and that this had perhaps influenced the England selectors.

It is of course the dream of any professional sportsman to represent his country and I truly believed at the time that I was the best wicket-keeper/batsman in the county game and that my chance to prove myself on the international stage was now overdue. If there was ever irrefutable proof that there was a 'keeper out there with safe pair of gloves and who could also bat a bit, then the Lord's game was surely it!

My performances can't have gone unnoticed as, in August, Trevor Ward and I were called up to play two England 'A' one-day internationals against Sri Lanka. At long last, I'd got my chance to show what I can do with three lions on my sweater. If I performed to my potential, I knew there was a place on the winter tour up for grabs and, to be fair, the games couldn't have gone better for me. Although they didn't have test status yet, Sri Lanka were packed full of their usual array of classy unpronounceables, including Mahanama, Tillekaratne, Jayasuriya and Aravinda de Silva, yet we beat them well in the first game. Batting first we posted 243 and I scored at a run a ball at the end of the innings to finish 26 not out. We bowled them out for 180 and I kept pretty well, not letting any byes through and taking a couple of catches. So far, so good.

We lost the second game but I chipped in another useful 28 not out at the end, kept tidily, let no byes through and caught their captain, Gurusinha. It was another decent performance and was about as much as I could have asked for. Finally I was starting to get some notices from the media, in particular from the *Daily Telegraph's* Christopher Martin-Jenkins, and all of a sudden my name was being touted for a place in the World Cup squad. Even more excitingly there was also talk of me being selected for the final test of the summer against the West Indies. The then England 'keeper, Jack Russell, was out of sorts and it was reportedly a toss up between myself and Alec Stewart. In the end the selectors went for Stewart, who'd only managed to scrape an average of seven-and-a-half in his two tests as a 'keeper against Australia, as they were desperate to pack the side with as much batting as possible. I firmly believe that if we'd been playing any team other than the fearsome West Indies, I would have been given my chance.

It wasn't to be, but I wasn't too downhearted as the touring squads were about to be announced and if I didn't make the main tour, I'd surely be jetting off with the England 'A' team. In those days there weren't any 'phone calls from the chairman of selectors politely asking if you'd do them the honour of sanding down your bat for a spot of winter cricket. You had to look it up on Teletext and that was it! On the day of the announcement I flicked on the telly and started to wade through the usual dross of celebrity recipes and pointless telephone surveys before reaching the cricket on page 990. For the main tour I was out of luck as, unsurprisingly, Russell and Stewart got the nod. This moment of mild disappointment mutated rapidly into stifling nausea when I found I'd also been omitted from 'A' tour, with Steve Rhodes and Warren Hegg coming from nowhere to be selected to go to the Caribbean. It was obviously, once again, a case of my face not fitting somewhere along the line and I was sick to the pit of my stomach that my chance of establishing myself as an international cricketer had to all intents and purposes disappeared. None of it seemed to make sense. Graeme Hick made 5 and 1 in those two England 'A' games and, despite his obvious and well-documented inability to come to terms with test cricket, was still being persevered with some ten years later. By comparison, I didn't let a single bye through and scored 54 unbeaten runs but was still immediately and unceremoniously binned as an international cricketer. Would somebody kindly show me the logic, please?

Once touring sides are announced, it's never normally the case that unlucky players are contacted to have the decision explained and their sensibilities cosseted. If you're in, you're in and if you're out, you're out. So it was with more than a modicum of disbelief that on the day after the announcement, I was told that Mickey Stewart was on the other end of the 'phone for me. Convinced that it was the usual Macca-style wind-up I picked up the receiver with a very facetious "evening Mickey", only to find it was indeed the England coach himself! He reassured me of his identity and informed me that for both touring parties it had been "a really close decision". Whether this watery platitude made it better or worse, I still haven't made up my mind. If ever there was a case of a miss being as good as a mile, this was it.

Being totally unprepared for the call, I was so taken aback that I couldn't think of any pertinent questions. My only retort, though not rude or abrupt, was 'Well that's life, isn't it?' He gave me the usual old flannel and told me to keep plugging away, but I greatly regret not asking him exactly what I had to do to get picked. I sincerely felt that my performances proved I was the best wicket-keeper in the county. I'd now got the exposure I had been lacking, so why wasn't I playing? Was my lifestyle not acceptable? Was I a "bad influence"?

It was a nice gesture by Mickey but I can't help thinking that he was, in reality, trying to salve his guilty conscience over a decision that he knew wasn't merit-based. Unfortunately, the mantle of "nearly-man" will always be a source of deep frustration for me as international recognition would have been the crowning moment of my career. If I'd been given that one chance and screwed up, then fine. At least I would have been offered an opportunity, however fleeting, to show what I could do. Not to be given that chance will forever leave me wondering how far I could have gone. Through each level of my career, I'd always started off as a relative also-ran. I'd always battle through and adapt my game with a pugnacious blend of application and attitude so that I *made* myself good enough. There's no reason to believe I couldn't make that same transition into international cricket. By not getting an international cap, I felt I'd broken the natural succession of Kent wicket-keepers into the England team. In not receiving the opportunity, I broke the dynasty started by Ames, Evans and Knott, even though my county record in terms of runs scored and catches taken is more than comparable.

I firmly believe that my loss was also very much England's loss, as I was one of those players who could flick themselves into another gear when the chips were down. A supporter at Tunbridge Wells summed it up perfectly when he came up to me and said 'Why is it that when Kent are 330 for three, you come in and can't get double figures, but when they're 130 for 5, you get 70 or 80?' Adversity and a tight situation always brought the best out of me, and it's that sort of pressure that is part and parcel of test cricket, and especially playing for England! James Allen of the *Kent Messenger* summed up the paradoxical manner in which I applied myself when he wrote: 'Give Steve Marsh a flat pitch and an attack that is at the end of its tether and you wonder if he's going to down tools and say he won't play. Only when presented with a challenge that most less determined individuals might shirk does Marsh seem really happy.'

What also bugged me was the selectors' almost blind preference for batsman/wicket-keepers. Keeping wicket is a highly specialist role and in a test-match environment it's a false economy to give the gloves to a part-timer in a desperate attempt to bolster a sagging batting line-up. At the highest level, you need to employ the best in every department. If a batsman/wicket-keeper misses a difficult chance to stump a Brian Lara or Steve Waugh early in their innings and the team concedes a hundred and fifty runs because of it, he'll have to go out and score a double hundred just to break even. World-class players will make you pay dearly for your mistakes, so a team has to give itself the best possible chance to dismiss them early.

This may infer criticism of that prime example of the species, Alec Stewart. In fact, I regard Alec as a very accomplished wicket-keeper in his own right who has improved immeasurably over the years. Yet while he may have kept very well in the fifth test against the West Indies, I have to say at the time I didn't think he was up to the job. These days, though, his athleticism standing back and alertness and agility standing up, make him a 'keeper of the highest quality.

The 'keeper for whom I had the most respect was Derbyshire's Bob Taylor. A highly accomplished practitioner of the art, he had the misfortune to always play understudy to Alan Knott in the England side. It turned out to be such a wait that the poor bloke went grey before he got his much warranted run in the team. Indeed Bob was one of a dying breed of quality English 'keepers. After the early nineties, when highly proficient performers like Jack Russell, Steve Rhodes and Jack Richards were all vying for England recognition, a mysterious talent vacuum began to develop. The lack of quality keeping options was highlighted by the recent selection of Chris Read, who in my view was thrust far too early into the England picture. Alas when Alec Stewart finally takes his leave, the stampede of mediocrity rushing to fill his boots will be deafening!

These days the institution of Kent nurturing world-class keepers from within the county has been broken. Disappointingly, it's the one tradition the committee seems to be able to dispense with. When I first became captain I advised the committee that they should start their search for my replacement as I felt the second team 'keeper, Simon Willis, wasn't quite good enough to keep wicket regularly at a first-class level. But it was a difficult situation as second eleven coach, Alan Ealham, was also Simon Willis' father-in-law. From a committee point of view, it was, therefore, a nettle too painful to grasp.

Kent should have already been grooming an eighteen year-old 'keeper who could have come in and pushed me hard over the last three or four years before I retired. Fortunately, I was still able to motivate myself and keep focused, so the lack of genuine competition for my place did not affect my performances.

With no youngster coming through, Kent then had to take the sad step of looking outside the county for a wicket-keeper for the first time. When they finally made the decision to bring in Paul Nixon for the beginning of the 2000 season, it was disappointing for me as I'd targeted that year as being my last full summer behind the stumps before I retired. I'd always said to myself that I wanted to go out with something still left to give, and the end of 2000, at the age of thirty-nine, would have been the perfect moment. It looked like my last hurrah in the first team was to be denied me.

I could understand the decision to bring Paul Nixon in when they did. Kent had nobody in the wings and he was available. Nevertheless, I would have been far happier if we'd been on an equal competitive footing for that final season. To have some real competition for the first time in years would have been just what I needed to finish my career on a high rather than going through the motions on the second team circuit. What's more, I was still a better 'keeper than Paul, and most of the team knew it. Numerous players have since come to me and said that, as a 'keeper, he wasn't in my league. So when he was named to go on the main England tour to Pakistan and Sri Lanka, you can imagine the cartwheels of unbridled joy I was turning!

For my final year I was asked to coach the second team and try and keep my eyes open for new wicket-keeping talent. It wasn't easy because the system in Kent is falling down at youth level. Not once was I ever asked by the county to run wicket-keeping seminars. Paul

Farbrace and I did in fact organise some coaching days purely for wicket-keepers ourselves, and that's how Simon Willis was spotted. At the moment the second team 'keeper is Geraint Jones, a Welsh-Australian, who has huge potential and should go a long way in the first-class game. Nevertheless his cosmopolitan ancestry amply illustrates the committee's refusal to invest in the future has heralded the unnecessary demise of a proud Kent tradition. The Kent committee loves tradition, but only when it suits them.

Being overlooked by England in 1991 was painful but I was determined not to allow the disappointment to scar me for life. At the time, Kent was an unfashionable county that was rarely challenging for honours and I certainly wasn't the only player to be overlooked. If I could have been more selfish with my personal goals, by putting international aspirations ahead of my county, then perhaps a cap could have come my way. But I knew I could never alter my core beliefs and chose instead to strive towards new challenges and objectives that were soon to be peeping their heads above the horizon.

Incidentally, my mark on the record books was not quite as indelible as I'd hoped. In the final of the Logan Cup in Zimbabwe in 1995/96, the captain and wicket-keeper of Matabeleland, Wayne James, dismissed nine Mashonaland Country Districts batsmen, catching seven and stumping two. Fortunately he did fall somewhat short of matching my unassailable feat of following up his record first-class haul with a century. He scored 99 in the first innings and 99 not out in the second!

FIVE

Four Lord's a weeping

To appear in a one day final at Lord's is a high-point in any cricketer's career, whether it be the NatWest Trophy, the Benson & Hedges Cup or even the National Village Knockout. During my career Kent reached the hallowed portals of cricket's head-quarters for six one-day finals and I was fortunate enough to play in four.

My first involvement with a Lord's final should have been in 1985 when we'd made it through to face Middlesex in the NatWest. In those days I was still alternating with Stuart Waterton for the first team spot when Alan Knott was not available. In the run-up to the game, Alan had been struggling with an injury and if he wasn't able to shake it off in time, it would be my turn to play. Having just finished a second team game at Usk, Graham Cowdrey and I were wheezing our way to Lord's in his asthmatic green Mini Metro and I was salivating profusely at the prospect of the ridiculousness of the selection policy actually working in my favour. All things being equal, I was only a few hours away from the most important day of my life. Then, out of the blue, Graham asked me what I'd do if Stuart Waterton was picked ahead of me for the final. A tidal wave of paranoia then washed over me. Did he know something I didn't? Did the possession of the name Cowdrey bestow on him some form of cricketing ESP? Stung by such an unpalatable suggestion I replied that if such an aberration were to come to pass, I'd throw a moody and walk straight out the ground.

On the day of the final we had taken our seats in the Mound Stand and half an hour before the scheduled start of play, the PA glibly crackled the numbing announcement that Stuart Waterton was replacing Alan Knott. I froze in my seat and began to grind my teeth furiously. How could they do this to me? Lord's bloody final or not, it was my turn! But with Julie sitting serenely at my side, it wouldn't have been appropriate for me to start throwing my toys out of the pram so I just sat there and fumed. Though I'm not proud to say it, I was honestly hoping Kent would get beaten that day, such was the bitterness of my disappointment.

As it turned out I got my wish and Kent were beaten. At the post match dinner at our hotel, I was still sullenly pushing my starter around the plate when our table was approached by the club treasurer, Tony Levick, who looked suspiciously like he'd slung one too many gins. In his inebriated state he attempted to commiserate with Laurie Potter and Kevin Jarvis and drivelled, 'Well, today boys, you were losers'. He then swung round unsteadily, fixed me in his gaze and continued, 'but I think *you're* probably the biggest loser of all'. I think Laurie could discern in my eyes the sort of look worn by Dr David Banner just before he turned into the Incredible Hulk, so he and Kevin ushered the idiot away before my eyebrows started to thicken and my shirt began to split. I've probably got a lot to thank them for because there's no doubt in my mind that I was totally prepared to get seriously up close and personal with this particular committee member. Brian Luckhurst then came up and, in a tone of conciliation that would have put Derek Nimmo to shame, tried to soften the blow by telling me that I was picked to go to Worcester the next day for a Sunday League game. Well whoopee do.

By the next season, Waterton was already on his bike, Knott had retired and I was now the county's first choice 'keeper. So barring plague or pestilence, the next time we made it to Lord's I'd be playing, no question. I didn't have to wait long as a narrow squeak of an eleven run victory in the semi-final of the Benson & Hedges Cup saw us through to meet Middlesex on 12th July 1986.

A final at Lord's is a totally different kettle of fish from the often tepid fare endured by players and supporters alike in the County Championship. From the moment you arrive at the ground on the Friday for practice, the atmosphere is electric. The television people and the press are swarming around you for interviews and the hairs on the back of your neck suddenly go into overdrive. Even my moustache was beginning to tingle!

Come the day of the game, the sheer volume of the crowds that greet you on your arrival at the ground from the hotel heightens the tension still further. But it wasn't until Mark Benson came back from the middle and told us that we were fielding that my rear end started to ponder making a unilateral declaration of independence. Knowing I was ten minutes away from walking out in front of 25,000 spectators and millions of armchair cricket fans, my stomach muscles knotted themselves tighter than the spring mechanism on a Roman siege catapult. I'm not an overly nervy guy, but I'd never felt anything like it before in my life.

But my time had come and it was do or die. I walked down two flights of stairs, across the Long Room and out onto the hallowed turf. I did my usual routine of getting the ball off the umpire and starting the warm-up. Alarmingly, my hand to eye co-ordination seemed to have undergone a most unwelcome temporary recalibration and nothing was going into my gloves properly. I felt as if I'd come out wearing someone else's kit and an ominous feeling of foreboding was starting to consume me. Surely I wasn't going to bottle it now, was I?

As the first over got underway, Graham Dilley sent one down the leg-side that flicked Wilf Slack's pads. Or was it Wilf Pad's slacks? I was still in such as state I couldn't be sure! To my eternal relief I dived like a salmon to my left snapped it up so cleanly that from that moment on I was completely focused and relaxed. To be honest, if the entire crowd had left during the remainder of the fifty-five overs, I wouldn't have noticed. The innings fairly flew by and I remember being pretty pleased with the first half of my afternoon's work, having taken either decent or excellent catches to dismiss the heart of the top order in Andy Miller, Mike Gatting and Roland Butcher. Having lost early wickets, Middlesex then started to get some runs on the board, with that fine old war-horse Clive Radley gradually easing himself to a half century. With his senior partner on 54, John Emburey played the ball half a dozen yards forward on the off-side, only to look up and see the forty-two year old veteran charging down the track towards him, calling for a run. Quick as a flash I scampered round from behind the wicket and amazingly managed to throw down the stumps at the other end to run him out. I say "amazingly" because most of my team-mates would tell you I've got the throw of a geek and couldn't hit Hadrian's Wall from ten yards. All of a sudden my premonitions of a day of hell began to dissipate.

With Richard Ellison taking 3 for 27 off his eleven overs we managed to restrict them to 199 for 7 off their allocation. It was a total that was at least thirty runs below par and we felt were in with a real chance. But in reply, the rot in our top-order batting set in even more quickly than usual as our first three batsmen, Benson, Hinks and Tavaré could muster only 17 between them. We'd slumped to 20 for 3 and the game looked up. The pressure of the situation then got to Neil Taylor, normally our most expansive batter, who could do little else than protect his wicket against the nagging accuracy of the England spin twins, Edmonds and Emburey. As a plague of dot balls began to infest the scorebook, we gradually started to fall behind the required rate. It wasn't until Graham Cowdrey came in and added 69 with Eldine Baptiste and 37 with Richard Ellison that we began to give ourselves a sniff of a chance. With Cowdrey eventually having holed out to Radley at deep mid-wicket off Simon Hughes for a superb 58, I was in with Graham Dilley needing 14 off the last over in the teeming rain.

As I thumped my bat down on the crease, wide-eyed and panting, waiting for the first ball, I knew that all things were still possible. Lord's is a relatively small ground and if I could lift the ball over the top, it had every chance of flying over the short boundaries either side of the wicket. I got the second away for two and then Simon Hughes bowled me a juicy full toss, which I swatted gloriously over square leg into the top tier of the Warner Stand for six. Now it was most definitely game on. Graham Dilley came down the wicket for a conference and suggested that, needing six to win, we could either run three twos or I could try and blast one out the ground again. For the fourth ball, Hughes bowled me a slower delivery. If I could have given it the kitchen sink one more time, I would have ended it there and then.

Whether it was Brearleyesque captaincy of the most cunning kind I don't know, but Mike Gatting left a tempting unguarded expanse in the third man area and, in an attempt to guide the ball down there, I agonisingly missed it altogether. Whatever was going to happen was out of my hands as the fifth ball was an excellent yorker which I just managed to squeeze out to point for a single. It was now up to Graham to hit a six off the last ball of the match. Anybody who saw his 56 playing second-fiddle to Ian Botham's titanic 149 not out against the Australians at Headingley in 1981 would be under no illusions that the boy Dilley knew how to hold a bat. Hughes was obviously going for another yorker but over-pitched and sent down a full toss instead. Graham uncoiled himself and launched into a huge cross-batted swipe but he didn't make full enough contact and the ball lobbed harmlessly out into the mid-wicket area. We could only come through for two runs, the same margin by which we lost the game. Graham then gave his off stump an almighty clattering and we both trudged off disconsolately.

Graham and I were perhaps guilty of being a little bit too Corinthian in our resolve to finish the game. Nobody would have blamed us if we'd come off as the rain and encircling gloom had turned the afternoon decidedly autumnal. Afterwards Mike Gatting made mention of our generosity: 'I would have understood totally if the Kent batsmen had come off because of the conditions. I can't say what I would have done because it didn't arise!' To be fair, when we put Middlesex in, we knew that there was a chance we'd be batting in the dark and it didn't help that we failed to complete our overs in the allotted time.

The mood in the dressing-room was predictably sober but to be honest it didn't last too long. It was only a matter of minutes before the club doctor Richard Collins (who was patching up Derek Aslett's toe after he'd sliced it open on a lager bottle) had a cooler bucket of ice and slush tipped over his head! It had been a superb final, I'd been mentioned in dispatches by match adjudicator David Gower and had loved every minute of it. I was still young and we had a very good one-day side, so there was no reason to suspect I wouldn't be back.

The wait was longer than expected as we didn't reappear at Lord's until 1992, when we faced Hampshire in my second B&H final. Mark Benson won the toss and put them in on what would turn out to be a relatively damp wicket. Though the Kent attack worked hard to contain Hampshire, the combination of lack of movement in the air and a wet ball gave the batting side the edge and Paul Terry and Tony Middleton put on a useful opening stand of 68. When Robin Smith and David Gower came together at 86 for 2, the combination of bludgeon at one end and rapier at the other added 85 in 20 overs and would lay the foundations of a challenging total of 253. A downpour during lunch had postponed the resumption until late afternoon and by the time play was called off for the day at 6.30pm, Kent were 4 for 0 off eight balls in reply.

With the game carried over, all of the big match atmosphere evaporated as soon as we were greeted the next morning by the sight of 18,000 empty seats. It was as if we had stumbled in on an agoraphobics' convention. Psychologically we were now at a huge disadvantage as the batting side feeds far more off the rhythm set by the spectators. The rush of adrenaline you feel after the massed ranks of your supporters roar their appreciation of a boundary is so inspirational that mentally it takes you to another level.

In reality Hampshire had already won the match on the Saturday night. We came out at ten o'clock on that almost surreal Sunday morning and raised the white flag quicker than a brigade of Italian conscripts in the Western Desert. The first 20 overs garnered a mere 43 runs, but at 116 for 2 in the thirty-fifth over, Benson and Carl Hooper suggested that the conclusion was not quite as foregone as first thought. Fighting cameos from Matthew Fleming, Graham Cowdrey and Mark Ealham, who dispatched Malcolm Marshall for a quite unbelievable six over long on, kept us in the hunt for while, but at no stage did we ever look favourites. Chasing ten an over, I was bowled by Shaun Udal for 7 and our last five wickets fell for 30 runs in four overs. We'd crumbled to 212 all out and were trounced by 41 runs.

Unlike the first final, when the drama of the day and our lion-hearted display made defeat almost palatable, this match had few redeeming features. I don't normally take any mental baggage with me once I leave the ground, but on this occasion the sense of dejection was almost overwhelming as Julie and I drove home down the M2 in a morose silence. We could take nothing whatsoever from this particularly disastrous Lord's final.

With Mark Benson injured for the 1995 B&H final against Lancashire, I proudly stepped up to the captaincy for the first time in a showpiece match. Although you could almost class me as a Lord's veteran by then, the weight of responsibility I felt in trying to alleviate the burden of expectation of the legions of success-starved county faithful seemed to render me back to the jelly-like state that characterised my first appearance nine years before. With the two best one day sides in the country in the final, inspired captaincy might just make the difference, so it was imperative I was on my mettle.

In 1997, John Wright and I were to get quite a taste for quirky motivational devices, but this year Daryl Foster decided to bring in that great county stalwart, Alan Ealham, for a good, old-fashioned call to arms. The day before the game Daryl got us all together and entreated him for some words of wisdom.

'Ealy, you've won finals with Kent before, whether it be the Gillette, Benson & Hedges or NatWest, and you've captained the side as well. What would you say to the guys?'

'Well, I'd treat it like another game,' mused Alan sagely, 'and go out and have me steak 'n' chips.'

Food for thought at the very least.

Taking the captaincy added an the extra dimension to my day and I was determined to milk the occasion for all it was worth. Walking out to the middle to toss up at Lord's for the first time must be a magical moment for all those who have experienced it. I'll certainly never forget the feeling of being able to bask in the national spotlight in the prime of my life in what is surely the nation's most ambient sporting arena.

Derek Ufton would have no doubt been very proud of me because I won the toss and decided to put Lancashire in. My opposite number that day was the affable Mike Watkinson. Mike was a guy with whom I'd always got on very well and he suggested very sportingly that whatever the result, the losing team should go to the opposition dressing-room for a post-match beer-up. It was not something that had ever happened before and I thought it was a great idea. Occasionally one or two members of the losing side might stick their head around the door, but for the whole team to tip up was unprecedented.

Having told the boys we were in the field I made my way to my corner of the dressing-room to get ready, which was something I didn't normally do until about fifteen minutes before we were due to go out. I went through my usual routine of whites, shirt, gloves and then blanched in abject horror on discovering that my pads were nowhere to be seen. I scattered the remnants of my coffin to the four winds but they were simply not there. The extent of the nightmare then dawned on me. Although all our kit had been brought over for practice, I wouldn't have needed my pads, so they were still in the boot of my car at the hotel. Well I supposed there was no real need to panic and I asked our twelfth man, Alan

Igglesden, if he wouldn't mind sprinting back to the Hilton International for me. Five minutes later he bounded breathlessly back into the changing room, minus the pads.

'Iggy, where are the pads?' I beseeched in a tone of voice that was teetering on hysteria.

'Sorry Marshy,' he winced, 'but I couldn't find the car.'

'What do you mean you couldn't find the fucking car! Has somebody nicked it?'

'Well, when the car park gets full, they start moving them around!'

A wicket-keeper walking out with batting pads on is something you'd see in the average under elevens match, but not generally in a Lord's final! It would only be marginally less embarrassing than when Bob Willis went out in a test match without his bat!

As I didn't have the stomach to do it myself, I then asked Iggy to have a word with the Lancashire 'keeper, Warren Hegg, to see if I could borrow his pads. It was lucky that I got on well with Heggy and it wasn't a problem. In his shoes I would have refused, just for the crack of it!

Crisis averted, I kept for the first hour in a pair of Heggy's Gray-Nicolls pads and, understandably, I got a rocket from my kit sponsor, Eurosport & Leisure. Having locked their product inside a car boot when it should have been lapping up its big moment in front of millions of would-be pad purchasers, I had to make sure I was wearing one of their boxes when I went round to explain!

If that episode gave me the first inkling that it wasn't to be our day, then the first ball of the morning made up my mind. Tim Wren bowled Michael Atherton a shortish one which he appeared to loft right down fine leg's throat. A sleepy Aravinda de Silva was the fielder, but when he finally woke up to the situation he ended up having to dive half a mile forward and only managed to get half a hand on the ball. If he had been concentrating it could have made all the difference as Atherton went on to make us pay with a typically gritty 93. By the time he was finally caught by David Fulton,

Lancashire had advanced to over two hundred and were on their way to posting 274, the second highest score in a B&H final.

When we had tossed it was pretty cloudy but by the time the Lancashire innings got started, the sun was breaking through and our bowlers lost the advantage of the conditions. There was little movement off the pitch and in the air and I was having a quiet time with no edges coming through. That's not to say, however, that the folks at home would have been unaware of my involvement in the game. It was the first year that they'd placed microphones behind the stumps and the techies in the TV editing suite would have doubtlessly enjoyed my earthy running commentaries. We're all familiar today with Alec Stewart's incessant chirping of 'oooh, I do like that Crofty', but in those days the novelty of the situation sometimes meant I forgot what a nice, polite, cultivated young man I was. So when the batsmen were getting on top, any lapses in the field received sharp admonishment from the skipper. Particularly embarrassing was the occasion when a ball was fired out towards Neil Taylor. Fine batsman though he was, Neil was never the sveltest of members of the Kent staff and, with the turning circle of the *USS Dwight D. Eisenhower*, he could occasionally be a bit of a liability in the field. With the pressure on, he let a regulation stop elude him so I hollered hoarsely, 'Chase the ball you fat twat!' This, I am told, reverberated through the country's living rooms causing several vicars to choke on their digestive biscuits. As a result I spent the next couple of overs making my apologies to the stump-mic.

So after the drama of forgetting my pads and coarsening the airwaves with my foul tongue, I now had the mammoth task of trying to get our troops somewhere close to 274. Our rookie opening batsman David Fulton saw this as his moment to get his name in the papers and strode out to the crease not in a helmet, but looking like the man from Del Monte in a large wide-brimmed sun-hat. Dave reckoned he had a theory. He believed that Wasim Akram was at his most dangerous when he was bowling a full length and would therefore goad him into bowling short by not wearing a lid. To be fair it appeared to work and Akram got wild enough to lose his line and length completely. Dave moved on confidently to 25 before he played across one and was trapped frustratingly LBW by Glenn Chapple.

On the matter of his head-gear, however, Dave and I beg to differ. We called him "Pheasant" because of the way he strutted around courting attention and I am convinced that the sun-hat ploy was nothing more than a pose for the benefit of any female viewers who might have switched on "possibly" in order to see Dave Fulton. As I say, he has his version and I have mine!

His self-cultivated image of suaveness personified when dealing with members of the opposite sex was put severely to the test after a representative game for the South of England against the North of England at Edgbaston. Why he admitted this particular aberration to us I will never know, but disclose it he did and therefore it must be shared! His confession runs like this: he was at an exclusive night-club called Liberty's and, as not infrequently happens, a fragrant young lady caught his eye. Despite him not wearing his magic sun-hat, the female in question was sufficiently beguiled by his tales of derring-do at the crease that she agreed to come back to the hotel for a cup of Gold Blend.

Being the considerate type, Dave bought her a drink at the hotel bar in a token effort to "get to know her" before they climbed the wooden hill to Bedfordshire. Having given her one of those "get yer draws off" looks similar to that afforded to Nicola Paggett by that slimy French bloke in the Cointreau commercial, the moment eventually arrived when Dave felt it was appropriate that they adjourn to more comfortable surroundings. Instead of the usual immediate acquiescence, the girl gave him a slightly peculiar look and asked him if he was really sure that it was what he wanted to do. Taken aback that this attractive young woman should suddenly turn so strangely coy, he whispered 'Of course it is,' as he gently tousled her silken locks, 'why ever shouldn't I?' As soon as he said it his blood turned cold as the light just caught her skin at a particular angle and he perceived the tell-tale hue of five o'clock shadow on her cheek! Despite assuring himself that this could not be happening, he knew he had to find out for sure what he was up against. In a Crocodile Dundee style manoeuvre he made a grab between his would-be partner's legs to ascertain whether he was indeed dealing with a bona fide Sheila. Well, "bona" was the operative word and Dave recoiled in abject horror as his hand encountered a very uninvited guest. Yes, he'd pulled himself a lady-boy! Like a cornered rat he didn't know whether to scream, punch him or run and hide. In the end he advised him that there had been a terrible mistake and that he'd an urgent appointment elsewhere.

Dave did pretty well telling the boys this one as he will never, ever live it down. He'd never be quite as cock sure again, that's for sure. I did tell him, however, that his secret was safe with me, I'd just put it in my book!

From ladies back to Lord's, where Trevor Ward and Neil Taylor went cheaply and the heart of our batting had been removed with only 80 runs on the board. Then Aravinda de Silva came in and played the most amazing knocks ever to grace cricket's Mecca. It was so swashbuckling in its execution that he would have made Errol Flynn look like Dame Edith Evans! With a panache that is rarely seen these days, Aravinda dispatched Akram, Chapple, Watkinson and Austin to all parts of the ground and won the admiration of every spectator who was lucky enough to witness it, Kent and Lancashire alike. From a hopeless cause, he and Graham Cowdrey turned the game on its head and somehow dragged Kent into a winning position. Then, just as the required run rate had been whittled down to a manageable level, David Shepherd triggered Graham Cowdrey out LBW in one of the worst decisions I had ever seen. For one thing his left leg was so far down the wicket it was debatable whether his front boot was still technically located in St John's Wood and, secondly, it was wider than a bus-load of spivs. Whether the label of being the country's supposed best umpire led him to believe he could see things other mere mortals couldn't, I don't know. What I

**Early days: Flowerpot
Man practising his
'keeping skills...**

Kent Messenger Group

**...experimenting with
facial hair...**

...and batting. *Kent Messenger Group*

Receiving my county cap from skipper Chris Cowdrey in 1986.

With four generations of 'keepers: Evans, Ames, Levett and Knott.

Anthony Roberts

**Mr Igglesden I presume?
Club patron the Duke of
Kent opens the extension to
the Ames-Levett sports
centre in 1995.**

**Iggy fails to
impress
Alec Stewart**

*Kent Messenger
Group*

| **Celebration...Graeme Hick goes back to the 'hut'.**

Ducking...
evasive action v. Essex.

...and diving!
Airborne in the NatWest Trophy v. Cambridgeshire.

Tom Morris

**Record day, no crowd!
Middlesex's Angus Fraser gives me
my eighth catch of the innings to
equal the world record at Lord's.
One more catch for the record out-right!**

**...alas it goes to Fleming at
slip. Congratulations to
Jazzer all the same.**

Tom Morri

**Monday ton: I follow up my
record with an unbeaten century.**

Do me a favour, Deano! *Anthony Roberts*

Tom Morris

Offering a prayer to the square-leg umpire!

Gower and Smith guide Hampshire to match wining total in the 1992 B&H Cup Final

The appeal of cricket!

Ady Kerry | **Graham Cowdrey's controversial LBW
seals our fate in the 1995 B&H final.**

Tom Morris | **Dynamic Duo.**
Teaming up with Graham Cowdrey
to dismiss Warwickshire's David
Thorne...
                                          ...and Andy Lloyd. | *Tom Morris*

'keeper v. 'keeper.
Tongue out for Russell.

tongue in!

**Marshy, do I not like
that!**

Tourists!
Despite another bad hair day, I enjoy a
beer with Chris Cowdrey in Barbados.

...and choir practice with
Jon Ayling and Robin Smith.

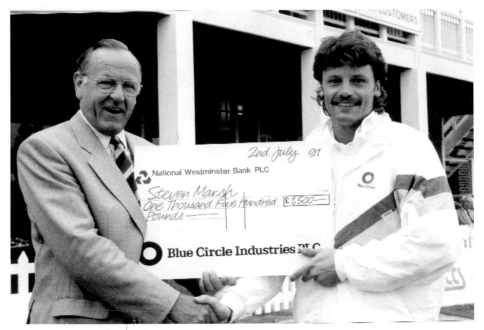

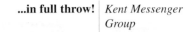

Kent Messenger Group | **Player of the month: cementing my relationship with the sponsors.**

Kent Messenger Group | **In full flow...**   **...in full throw!** | *Kent Messenger Group*

Kent Messenger Group **Anybody fancy a pyjama party?**

Anthony Roberts

Kent v. Sri Lanka. Passing the time of day with Aravinda de Silva.

Anthony Roberts

Top: Attack...

Kent Messenger Group

Bottom: ...and defence!

Kent Messenger Group

**The gloves are off!
Bidding my farewells
in my last appearance
at Canterbury.**

Clan Marsh.

do know is that it lost us the game. With Graham now departed, the pressure on Aravinda was now intense and his shot making became even more outrageous as he single-handedly tried to guide us to victory. It must have been a bridge too far when with six wickets down I made my way out to join him. Out of our partnership of 34, the Sri Lankan pocket-battleship had made 30 by the time he holed out to Graham Lloyd off Ian Austin for 112. I seemed to lose my focus for an instant and was caught by John Crawley next ball and the innings eventually petered out in the fifty-third over with Kent still needing another 35 runs. Stuffed again.

Having built all our hopes around Aravinda, I was disappointed that we capitulated so easily after he was dismissed. Where was the Steve Marsh who never knew the meaning of defeat? It was as if we were collectively cowering with our eyes shut waiting for the coup de grace. We'd had our backs against the wall on plenty of occasions previously and still managed to prevail, but the pernicious influence of the Lord's hoodoo seemed to sap our strength both mentally and physically just at the crucial moment.

True to my word, I led the boys into the Lancashire dressing-room. The knife was twisted one more time as the scene of unbridled jubilation that greeted us underlined what it meant to win one of these trophies. And I'd now lost three. The days of going to Lord's for a nice day out were long gone. I was now there for the sole purpose of winning and my repeated failure to do so was nudging me towards the low point of my career.

If I were ever to turn on *Sesame Street* to be told that the programme was be being brought to me by the letters 'B' and 'H', i'm positive I'd break out into a cold sweat. Nevertheless it was with my usual chirpy optimism that I approached my fourth final in that competition in 1997. It was Kent's sixth fifty-fifty chance of picking up a Lord's trophy since 1978 and the law of averages was screaming that success was a statistical certainty. Unfortunately it doesn't quite work like that. One roulette player in Monte Carlo once noted that black came up twenty-eight times in succession, so by that reckoning we could still be gong-less by the middle of the twenty-first century! But the omens were good. We were in the middle of our best season for two decades and we were playing a team, Surrey, whom we'd comprehensively beaten in the preliminary stages. Team spirit was excellent and we feared absolutely nobody. Who could possibly piddle on our chips now?

At this stage I was settled in my role as captain and had a fair idea of where we had gone wrong in previous finals. Too many players had been caught up by the occasion and spent more time worrying about incidentals like where great aunt Flo would be sitting rather than focusing on the task of winning.

I'd been reading some of Will Carling's musings on team motivation and I decided there was no reason why they couldn't be translated into a cricketing context. One golden rule was to set the winning of the competition as the sole objective, not simply making the final. In the rugby world cup, England had been so chuffed at making it to the final that they forgot to come out and play against Australia. Our boys seemed to be in the same frame of mind. When you get to a quarter final it's tempting to tell them they're only two games away from Lord's. This year I was telling them that they were just three games away from winning it.

Another psychological trick I took off Carling was to write each player an individual note and push it under their doors the night before the game - a sort of Carling white label, if you like! It let them know that everything had been taken care of and reassured them of why they had been picked. Even international cricketers like Paul Strang were very appreciative of the gesture and if nothing else, I now believed they were focused on the job in hand.

Although the morning of the final was very overcast, I had looked back through the records and saw that in the last seven finals, the side batting first had won on six occasions. From my own bitter experience I knew that winning the toss and fielding first was a losing formula. When you unsuccessfully chase a total three times on the trot, you start to get a little paranoid, so I thought it was time we changed our luck a little. After all, the early morning conditions for batting are far more benign in July than they are in September for the NatWest, so I couldn't see a problem with us going out and setting a target for a change. Anyway, the coin went up at 10.30 and I duly won the toss. There was an almost audible groan of disbelief when it was announced that I'd chosen to bat in such dreary conditions. I knew it was a bit of a gamble but when I'd spoken to Ian Botham before the toss and told him what I had planned, he told me it would be a fair call.

My punt seemed to have paid off when at five to eleven the sun decided to get his hat on. In the end, however, we put up a below par total of 212 for 9 off the new allocation of fifty overs. The fact that we fell thirty or forty runs short had less to do with the conditions and more to do with bad luck and eccentric umpiring. Martin Bicknell had been bowling a poor line but the centurion of the quarter final, Matthew Walker, still managed to drag a probable wide back onto his stumps. Then David Shepherd did us one of his favours next ball when he sent Matthew Fleming back with another poor LBW decision. Trevor Ward and Alan Wells soon followed in quick order, victims of more dubious LBWs, and all of a sudden we found ourselves up to our neck in quicksand at 68 for 4. I could almost sense a lynch mob of Kent members gathering at the bottom of the pavilion steps.

The seventh cavalry in the form of the middle order galloped along to save my scalp as Nigel Llong and Mark Ealham, who'd obviously had their steak and chips the night before, played responsible knocks of 42 and 52 respectively to go some way to rescue the innings. Paul Strang and I then chipped in with useful contributions towards the end to at least give the bowlers something reasonable to bowl at. On a good wicket in the semi-final at Canterbury we'd only posted 206 but still managed to beat Northamptonshire by 66 runs. So we knew we had the necessary firepower.

Hope almost turned into optimism at the start of the Surrey reply when, off the fourth ball of the innings, Matthew Fleming brilliantly plucked out of the air Alistair Brown's full-blooded cut to square cover. Alas, from that point on it became the Ben Hollioake story as the nineteen-year-old played one of only two truly memorable innings anyone's ever seen him complete. It was unfortunate that our bowlers proceeded to serve him up his match-winning innings on a plate. Despite boasting an attack that consisted of McCague, Headley, Ealham, Fleming and Strang - all of them international cricketers at one stage or another - we sent down a malevolent pot-pourri of half-volleys, long-hops and no balls that simply yelled out to be punished. However I mixed it up, the result always was the same: leg-side half-volley and four runs to Hollioake. He and Alec Stewart gratefully accepted the gifts to put on 159, and by the time the youngster had chipped Mark Ealham to mid-on just two short of his century, the game was over. Stewart and Graham Thorpe wrapped up proceedings with five overs to spare to give Surrey a thumping eight wicket victory. In previous finals we had often flattered to deceive, but on this occasion we weren't even at the races. We'd short-changed ourselves and the long-suffering members once again. I just couldn't understand it. The more finals we played, the worse it seemed we were getting hammered.

Perhaps Alan Ealham had been right back in 1995. Maybe we did get too wrapped up in ourselves, too analytical, too up tight. Maybe we should have just gone out there and played. All easier said than done, of course. One thing was for sure though, Kent and Lord's finals just did not mix. It was doubly frustrating for me personally because, as far as I was concerned, the needle was starting to get dangerously close to empty and it looked as if I were to be denied that crowning moment. I had a feeling I wouldn't return to Lord's and that is how it turned out. As Benson & Hedges make Hamlet cigars, you would have thought they could have sent me a case out of sympathy. You could have almost made *Air on the G String* my theme tune!

SIX

It's a jungle out there

Since my early days, one of the ways the game has changed for the worse has been the growing tendency for teams not to mix socially after the stumps had been drawn. After the close of play in the eighties and early nineties, oppositions used to have a drink on at least one of the nights they were away. You would meet up in the bar and talk about whatever took your fancy and along the way you'd pick up a lot of valid, useful information. Nowadays, in an effort to be more professional, teams will shoot straight out of the ground making a bee-line for the hotel. When this happens you lose, firstly, the potential to pick up hints and tips from great players and, secondly, the opportunity to diffuse any incident that may have occurred over the course of that day's play. All sorts of niggles have been allowed to fester into something more serious, merely because the two players involved have not been able to get together and patch it up afterwards over a Bacardi Breezer.

A case in point was when we were playing Yorkshire at Maidstone. Just after lunch, Richard Stemp took issue with me over something - he probably didn't like my batting (not many people do) - and a rolling confrontation developed that flared up again after tea. We managed to keep away from each other's throats until the close of play but bumped into each other again in the bar. Our contretemps could have easily re-ignited, but instead of standing there and pointing fingers, we bought each other a beer and smoothed it all over. We were never going to feature too highly on each other's Christmas card lists or anything, but from that moment we developed a mutual respect that would continue for several seasons.

I can also recall having a lively exchange with Essex's Australian all-rounder Stuart Law one afternoon at Ilford. We were ticking along quite nicely at 400-odd for six when Law decided to administer first-team rookie, Julian Thompson, a dose of grade 'A' Aussie invective. As the senior batsman in the partnership I tried to lend some moral support and the tactic obviously worked because Law quickly swung his gunsight onto me.

'How much fucking longer are you going to be batting?' he asked with that antipodean twang so cherished by lower order batsmen up and down the country.

'Well as long as you're bowling,' I retorted, 'I'm staying out here!'

It all carried on in a similar vein up to tea, occasionally getting quite lively. By the time it was Mr Law's turn to bat in the Essex innings, we were all geared up for a bit of fun. He'd spent most of his knock cussing and generally slating English cricket, so, as Min Patel was coming in to bowl, I turned to Carl Hooper at slip and said in a pantomime whisper:

'Carl, which three bowlers in the world do you most like facing? And that obviously doesn't include Stuart Law, who's top of everyone's list.'

Law turned away from wicket muttering and I chipped in mischievously, 'Oh Stuart, terribly sorry, can you hear that?'

Later on it got quite nasty, but once we got into the bar and had a drink, the situation was diffused. For the next two or three games that Stuart and I played against each other, we continued to be very amicable.

The trick of playing on batmen's nerves by talking *about* them rather than *to* them was something I'd picked up from the past-masters of the psychological game, the Australians. Sledging is normally assumed to be a strictly mano-a-mano confrontation laced with swearing, glaring and gesticulation, but the Aussies noted the administrators' distaste of personal intimidation and would adopt far more subtle tactics. Instead of directing their snide remarks straight at their prey, they would talk about him in the third person, pretending he wasn't there. As a batsman, you have no come-back. If you decided to interfere, they would request in no uncertain terms that you didn't interrupt their private conversation.

I only played the Australians a couple of times, but I learnt a great deal. As a wicket-keeper I was in the ideal position to re-employ some of those tactics. A good example of us putting those lessons successfully into practice was the wicket of Derbyshire's Simon Base a few seasons ago. A couple of months previously he'd been bowling at me at Derby when I snicked one through to the 'keeper and didn't walk. I was never plagued with too many qualms of guilt or sentimentality in those situations as, in the professional game, I always tended to stand my ground and let the umpire earn his corn. I got away with it but then, quite rightly, faced some harsh questioning of my parentage from the bowler and close fielders. Anyway, as these are the realities of modern cricket, I took my medicine and got on with game. Then came the day that we were playing Derbyshire at Canterbury and right from the off Mr Base really tore into me. In my book, each new game should be a clean sheet of paper, but on this occasion he wasn't having any of it. So when it was his turn to bat, I decided to mete out some retribution. I struck up some banter with Mark Benson at slip and Chris Penn at silly point about Base's inability to come to terms with our orthodox left armer Richard Davis and suggested that his batting was an embarrassment and that he should do himself and his team a favour by getting out. With that he turned round.

'Do you realise, I can hear that?'

Tickled that he'd risen so easily to the bait I replied,

'For one, you were supposed to, and secondly I'm talking to my mates, so don't butt in my conversation!'

He then issued me with a chill warning of an impending day of judgement.

'Well, just remember it's a long season.'

My reply of 'But we're not playing you again this season!' raised his blood pressure to such a level that he completely lost it. Two balls later he charged four yards down the wicket, missed the ball by a couple of feet and was comprehensively stumped. The three of us around the bat took great delight in knowing that that wicket was achieved purely by a nifty piece of psychology.

When the boot was on the other foot and I was keeping to a batsman who refused to walk, I was never hypocritical enough to blame him for doing so. It didn't, however, prevent me from dishing out plenty of stick. Again, I avoided the use of the expletive and just concentrated on the mind games strategy. At the end of the over I'd walk past the guilty party and say 'I used to think you were a good man, now I know you're not' or 'I had a lot of respect for you but that's gone. Don't even think about having a drink with me after the game'. This wasn't the case as I'd always have a jar with them afterwards, but occasionally the deepness of the crimson hue they adopted betrayed how tightly you'd got them by the psychological short hairs.

On one extreme there were those metaphor-mixing shrinking violets who were just lambs to the slaughter, and on the other there was select group of players you definitely wouldn't want to mess with. A notable member of this latter category was David Smith, the burly Surrey batsman. He was an aggressive character on the cricket field who was always pumped up and ready for a ruck. Misdemeanours included him having a fight outside The Oval with Ian Greig and being demoted to the second team after knocking a stump out of the ground with his bat after having been run out by us in the Sunday League! So trifle with him at your peril.

David's notoriously low irritability threshold was laid bare in a championship game at Tunbridge Wells. We all thought he had knicked one behind but he stayed rooted to the crease and was given not out. The bowler, Alan Igglesden, came marching down the track with the usual sort of friendly advice for batmen who chose to stand their ground. David retorted venemously, 'Look, I didn't fucking hit it, alright?' and made a point of showing Iggy the bat, just in case he'd failed to get the message. He then swung straight round to me and barked, 'And don't you start to even contemplate fucking saying anything'. I didn't utter a word!

Things could occasionally get a little boisterous in the heat of the moment, although Smithy and I can both see the funny side looking back on it now.

There was always the occasional player whose fragility of temperament would lead him to self-destruct without any exterior influence whatsoever. A serial practitioner of the "Tasmanian Devil" syndrome was Derbyshire's Danish seamer Ole "Stan" Mortensen. Stan was a quality performer who could beat you all ends up if the pitch conditions were in his favour, but on the cricket field I'm sure his lift didn't go quite all the way to the top floor.

We were playing them at Chesterfield in a Sunday League game, and in the days before it was regarded as a commonplace to promote someone up the order to slog early runs, I was sent in to open as a pinch-hitter. I could only think that the rarefied atmosphere of the top of the order got to me because I couldn't lay a bat on anything Mortensen served up. Admittedly, a bouncy, seaming wicket with the Viking at one end and Michael Holding at the other was hardly the optimum pinch-hitting environment, but I nevertheless decided to play shots from ball one.

The first over from the Dane consisted of six swipes and six misses. Holding then bowled out a maiden to Mark Benson and off the third over I left the first one and then played and missed at the next four. Off the last ball I tried yet another expansive shot only to slice once more through thin air. This was obviously was the last straw for poor Stan and a small nuclear device seemed to then go off in his head. He stood in the middle of the wicket, turned to the crowd, stretched out both his arms to the heavens and at the top of his voice yelled 'Fuck me hell-fire!!'. Whether this was an ancient Norse oath, I'm not totally sure, but it certainly caused no little amusement among the paying public. Apparently, "hell-fire" was a suffix that he regularly used in conjunction with expletives of varying extremity. I'm led to believe that the "fuck me" prefix was reserved for situations at the more stressed end of the emotional spectrum. The mood was further enlivened when he stumbled down the wicket towards me pretending to be a blind man with a white stick shouting in his amusing Scandinavian accent 'Whad do you theenk you're faarking dooing?' It certainly didn't do my reputation as a pinch-hitter much good.

My various antics behind the stumps failed to endear me to the majority of opposition players and there were times when my on-field popularity rating struggled to make it above ankle height. It didn't particularly bother me as most people knew that I was perfectly sociable off the field, although on it I was prepared to win at any cost, as long as it was above-board and within the laws of the game. I was a professional and had a job to do, it was as simple as that.

We were once at Canterbury against Essex, a side against whom we'd had a couple of lively run-ins over the previous couple of seasons. With it being a local derby, there was normally something going on, and after one such altercation, Paul Grayson, who was batting, turned round to me and said, 'What's it like to be the most hated man in county cricket?' I didn't know whether such an accusation was supposed to make me shrivel up into a hysterical, sobbing ball, but he actually played right into my hands. 'Well I take that as an absolute compliment,' I responded gleefully, 'I now know damn well that you and your mates up there are too scared stiff to come out!' I was pretty skilled in turning most things around to my advantage, and even if he didn't mean literally I was hated, I was quite happy to take it in the spirit it wasn't intended.

Over the years, sledging has developed into almost an art form and if you ask around at most counties you can unearth some classic confrontations. One of my favourite stories concerns the two Allans, Donald and Lamb, and was related to me by the then Warwickshire captain, Dermot Reeve. Warwicks were playing Northants at Edgbaston and Allan Donald was bowling at the speed of light on a blisteringly quick wicket. Allan Lamb came out to bat and first ball Donald tried to pitch it up and bowl him through sheer pace. Lamb, who ate and drank quality fast bowling, then proceeded to dispatch it masterfully to the cover boundary. Probably out of deference to their shared homeland, Donald acknowledged the shot, span on his heels and went back to his mark. Next ball was slightly short of a length, but this time Lamb rocked back and punished it again through the cover area for four. Smarting from the dismissiveness of his treatment, Donald then produced a vicious bouncer for the third ball which Lamb did very well to avoid as it hurtled past him towards Keith Piper's gloves, some thirty-five yards back. Buoyed at having stopped the rot, Donald forgot his previously impeccable manners, strode down the wicket and calmly advised Lamb, 'You fucking drive cars and that's it'. After the short one, the old two card trick dictated that the next ball was the block-hole delivery. As always with the best-laid plans, it ended up being a juicy half-volley. Having smashed him through the covers for a third time, Lamb walked up the wicket for a nose to nose confrontation with the great fast bowler and retorted 'Park that fucker then!'

A boil that has burst onto the sporting public's consciousness in the last few years has been the saga of ball tampering. In discussing this topic, it's necessary to establish one very important premise: all counties tamper with the ball to a greater or lesser extent. The old trick of putting lip-ice on one side of the ball is now pretty much old hat. Technology has moved on and has now become a little more covert. Nowadays, the fashion is to use the sugar in sweets to generate the shine. It's not against the laws of the game to take a bag of mint imperials out with you and we'd have a rota, with one player designated to suck 'em and see for a dozen or so overs. It had to be on a rota basis, because if one guy alone was allocated the job, it wouldn't be two years before he'd be retired out of the game with diabetes, gum disease, chronic weight problem and teeth like a bowl of cornflakes!

It didn't always go quite according to plan. We were preparing for one game at Canterbury when I asked who'd got the 'bugs (slang for humbugs). Realising we hadn't got any, I dispatched our twelfth man, Chris Walsh, to the nearest confectionery stand. Now bearing in mind that there was one essential ingredient that did the trick, I was less than impressed when he tipped up, looking very pleased with himself, with several packs of sugar free gum! He was obviously on a different "orbit" to the rest of us.

In fact Chris laid further claim to the title of Britain's most useless twelfth man in an incident at Canterbury in '97. It was in the days when drinks carts were in the process of superseding the traditional tray of Dan Maskell's favourite tipple, Robinson's Barley Water. In a watershed for the game as we knew it, our mid-session glucose impregnated sustenance was now being brought out to us in a perambulator type contraption. Now Chris was an Old Tonbridgian and therefore not short of a GCSE or twelve, but in terms of general street-wise nous, he was bereft. He was, bless him, the sort of bloke you could send off to find a spirit level bubble or a long-wait. On this occasion I suggested to him to fill up his Peugeot 205 with the drinks, dismantle the perimeter advertising hoardings, move the water-whale out of the way, then drive on and open up the boot so we could all sit down and have a drink!

I never thought for a minute that he'd go for it, but sure enough, come the drinks interval, back went the boards and onto the outfield trundled this Peugeot 205 (though it should have really been a Lada for all the provisions it was storing) and parked right outside the committee room! Like a good public schoolboy he must have thought that if he didn't obey the head prefect, he'd be caned! So we strolled over and got our drinks and one of their batsmen even ended up inspecting his nasal hair in the passenger side vanity mirror! The crowd were really seeing the funny side but the old duffers outside the committee room were incandescent. I later spared Chris being hauled over the coals by admitting my complicity in the matter and I don't think the poor guy took anything I said seriously ever again!

The phenomenon of reverse swing occurs in two ways, either naturally or by ball doctoring. The subversive approach involves the fielding side making one side of the ball heavier than the other through the application of moisture. The Pakistanis then developed the procedure by picking the seam or quarter seam. Seam picking aside, I don't have a problem with that sort of approach. It's your ball for a hundred overs and as long as you respect the general integrity of the ball, you should be permitted to do what you want with it. It would certainly cut out a lot of the grey areas that bowlers, captains and umpires have to contend with. Technically speaking, shining the ball is tampering with it, so where do you draw the line?

It's one thing developing reverse swing, but it's another controlling what can often be a double-edged weapon. Waqar Younis is an absolute master, as is Darren Gough. Philip DeFreitas told me once that in one overseas test, Goughie was almost unplayable from one end with reverse swing, whilst from the other he couldn't control it and took a frightful hammering. So it's alright for an individual to have the knack, but it's far better if the whole attack can exploit it as a unit.

The Pakistani bowler we respected the most was without doubt Wasim Akram. His ability to generate bursts of fearsome pace put the fear of Allah into some of our less technically adept lower-order batsmen. It didn't matter what condition the ball was in, he could destroy batsmen with a well-directed sneer. Although the fear factor was never an issue for me, I do remember being none too popular with certain tail-enders who used to have to pick up the tab for some of my antics when the likes of Wasim were in full flight.

There was one particular Benson & Hedges match at Old Trafford when my Wasim-baiting almost caused Alan Igglesden to register medical science's first case of *pre*-traumatic stress disorder. Wasim, fired up and bowling at ten tenths hostility, sent an unplayable outswinger down to me and went up screaming for a catch behind. I was nowhere near good enough to get any willow on it and was correctly given not out, much to the fury of the bowler. Basically, Wasim went berserk and came down the track to exchange views. True to the usual script he called me a "fucking cheat" and I told him to go and look in the mirror. All good clean fun and certainly nothing out of the ordinary for a Tuesday afternoon in Manchester.

Although we subsequently became good mates, Wasim was not a happy camper. The red mists descended in a similar fashion to when Dave Fulton came out to greet him in his Wilfrid Hyde-White hat in the 1997 B&H final. The more riled he became, the faster he bowled and the shorter he dropped it. I just stood there either flat-batting him through mid-wicket for four or cutting him away over the top of point. I even top-edged him over the slips for six!

Back in the pavilion, Iggy was next in and the guys reckoned that they'd never seen a batsman in such a pitiful state of terror. The side-on angle of the pavilion accentuated the brute force with which Wasim was launching his projectiles and Iggy had an all-too clear view of how the Pakistani pace-man was notching up the warp factor with every streaky shot I played. Apparently he was walking up and down the balcony grizzling 'What's that twat Marshy up to, keep winding him up? Doesn't he know I'm the fucker who he's going to be taking it out on?' Luckily for Iggy he was spared the confrontation as Tony Merrick and I won the battle and Wasim trudged off to the boundary for a blow.

To be fair, nobody ever fancied facing Wasim, not even the top order, and they certainly didn't need me stirring the pot! Fast bowlers have pretty long memories and the next time we played Lancashire it was pay-back time for all of us!

Another player to carry the can for my on-field lippiness was Graham Cowdrey. Batting together against Sussex at Canterbury, Graham and I were having the luck of the Irish against the giant

South African, Garth Le Roux. Try as he may, he simply couldn't find the edge and was getting increasingly arsey, chuntering back insults in his yarpy Springbok accent after practically ever delivery. After making Graham play and miss at two on the trot, Garth's constant whining had got too much for me and, as he made his way back past me at the non-striker's end, I let fly: 'I've just about had enough of this. Why don't just get back to your fucking mark and bowl?' Garth swung round and, believing the remark had come from the batsman, stared at Graham long and hard with his steely blue eyes and retorted 'Han waa don't yoo git on with your fuckin' battin', fatty?!' Dumped right in it, Graham stood there non-plussed while I just sat on my bat, stared innocently towards the heavens, nonchalantly whistling myself a ditty!

Waqar Younis was also a fearfully tricky customer. He wasn't as quick as Wasim but his control and ability to swing a ball in late made him almost unplayable in certain conditions. Trevor Ward and Mark Benson used to say that the best time to face Waqar was with the new ball because he did less with it. Once it had scuffed up, it was usually the poor guys lower down the order who'd get blown away. Against Surrey at Canterbury I witnessed Waqar at his rampaging, destructive best. I was the non-striker when the left-hander Chris Penn came out to join me. First ball up, Waqar pitched a full-length delivery on Chris' leg stump, which swung away at the last instant to remove his off peg leaving him utterly bemused. I was out there again when Chris came out for his second knock. He took guard and Waqar tore in and did exactly the same thing again. A king pair and Chris really didn't have a prayer on either occasion. It turned out to be a pretty awesome display that served to prove how a world class bowler can turn a game on its head in just a few super-charged overs. From coasting to a comfortable win, we were in danger of losing after a single spell of Waqar carnage. It wasn't long before my middle stump was also cartwheeling its merry way back to Nackington Road and we barely held out for a draw.

Looking down the batting order, there was almost a sliding scale of apprehension when a top-drawer fast bowler started to mark out his run-up. The top two thirds of the order were nervous about being unable to cope with their quality, while a few of the rabbits used to dissolve into quivering wrecks. Personally, I never minded facing the quicks. I certainly wasn't frightened, not even apprehensive. I'd come a long way since that day in 1981 when Kent's second team coach, Colin Page came up to me and said 'It's a lucky thing you're a decent 'keeper Steve, because your batting's abysmal!'

Luckily, you can get used to most things - even the sight of Curtly Ambrose, elbows flailing, bearing down on you at full tilt. Like anything, the more you face, the easier it becomes. The first technique you have to learn is self-preservation, from there everything else is a bonus! Decisiveness is the key. So many batting injuries occur because the batsman gets caught in two minds whether to duck or sway out of the way of a bouncer. They end up slumped in some in some semi-pathetic stoop and all of a sudden it's clunk, goodnight Charlie! Admittedly, you don't have time to bake a cake, but you do get just enough to formulate your plan. As the ball leaves the bowler's hand you can generally pick what length it's going to be and it's then a case of adjusting your feet and getting into line. The fatal error is, however, to try and second-guess the bowler's intentions. If you're daft enough to bat by numbers, it's highly likely that sooner rather than later you'll duck into a decent length delivery having already convinced yourself that a short-pitcher was inevitable. You've got to somehow put the game of bluff, double-bluff and triple-bluff out of your mind and play each ball on its merits. Easier said than done, I know.

Facing the quicks, there's never a moment's respite. Even if you play them perfectly and respectfully out of the middle of the bat, they're straight back at you with some form of psychological subversion. Malcolm Marshall was a particularly wily customer. I'd flourish a neat forward defensive back along the track to him and he'd just stare back at me, smile and shake his head. He'd then shout

'Hey, cappy!' and enter into an extravagant dialogue with Mark Nicholas about the price of fish. Even though he'd be bowling juicy away-swingers, he'd then take a slip out and move him just behind square on the leg-side. I'd stand there thinking to myself 'God, he's worked me out. He knows exactly how he's going to get me!' and from being relatively comfortable, I'd all of a sudden become riddled with doubt and paranoia. Eventually I'd learn that the most effective counter-measure was to go for a walk and stand on your bat at square leg between deliveries!

You wouldn't even have time to do that if you were facing Worcestershire's Tom Moody, as his favourite ploy was to fire one down before you were ready. All batsmen have individual routines they perform prior to each delivery and it can be most disconcerting to have one whizzing past your left ear while you're standing there still adjusting your box! It was a cheekily effective tactic and on more than one occasion he was onto me so quickly that I had no time to back away and was forced into playing a false shot.

Of the few top quality spinners I faced through my career, the pick had to be Surrey's Saqlain Mushtaq, although I did manage once to spank him for 24 in one over in a B&H game. One of the most impressive displays of spin I witnessed didn't actually occur during a game, but in the nets at Canterbury. It was in 1995 when Aravinda de Silva came to the ground to meet us for the first time. As he strolled across the outfield we could see he had this peculiar guy trailing behind him carrying his bags. Up in the dressing-room Mark Benson introduced Aravinda to us all while his bag boy, who could easily have been mistaken for Sri Lanka's answer to Mr Bean, stood quiet as a church mouse in the corner. We all got changed and went out for a net while Aravinda's little chum just stood there in his civvies and looked on. Next day, same thing. Aravinda walks across the ground pursued by this young guy, semi-submerged by half a ton of kit. While we were getting changed, Aravinda asked Mark if his friend would be allowed to have a bowl in the nets. Not wishing to upset his new recruit, Benny agreed. Having borrowed some kit, the "bag boy's" opening deliveries turned a yard and it wasn't long before he'd completely bamboozled half the batsmen in the club. Frustrated that they couldn't pick him, they were charging down the track and embarrassing themselves hopelessly. He was virtually unplayable! Naturally the guys were intrigued to find out his identity and Aravinda merely shrugged his shoulders and said 'Well, although he's played a couple of tests he's fairly new on the scene. His name's Muralitharan.'

Apart from getting out LBW a disproportionate number of times, my main weakness was my lack of concentration. On a flat wicket I'd occasionally drift off for a second and play a silly shot. I seldom cashed in when the conditions were in my favour. I'm sure I could have improved on my career first-class average of 28 if I'd shown a little more application and even been a bit more selfish in the way I played. But for me cricket is a team game and I wasn't prepared, like some players, to jealously protect my average when the match situation dictated I may need to sacrifice my wicket.

10,000 runs in first-class cricket wasn't a bad return for somebody once rated "abysmal". It confirmed my belief that cricket's a game played 90 per cent in the mind as I gradually overcame my technical deficiencies through a positive mental attitude to become a respectable middle order performer.

In nearly twenty years of first-class cricket, I've seen plenty of bizarre dismissals and have lost count of the number of times the ball has hit a stump and failed to dislodge a bail. In my final season I played a second team game at Taunton and witnessed a particularly galling way for a batsman to lose his wicket. Our new signing Ben Trott was bowling and Dave Fulton at second slip looked to have a straightforward edge under control when he spilled it. Somehow he managed to get his right boot under it, juggled it three times, before flicking it up and catching it. As a batsman, that's when you know it's not going to be your day.

Probably even more unfortunate was Glamorgan's Hamesh Anthony in 1995. Glamorgan were making a very useful fist of chasing a target of 271 at Tunbridge Wells when Anthony drove a Martin McCague half-volley so forcefully down the ground that it hit, and almost pole-axed, umpire Allan Jones. Having set off in keen anticipation of some runs, the batsman froze as the ball cannoned off Jones to Martin who lobbed the ball back to me to run out the unfortunately stranded Welshman. The match ended up as a draw.

On another occasion we were playing Oxford University at Oxford when Matthew Fleming got himself out in similarly peculiar circumstances. Being the shot-maker he is, his eyes obviously lit up at the prospect of hooking some spotty undergraduate's long-hop for six over square leg. So healthy was his enthusiasm to capitalise on such a generous invitation, he played the shot so early that he missed the ball on his first swipe and then dollied it gently to second slip off the back of his bat as he came round a second time to complete his follow-through.

With a bat in his hand, Matthew Fleming can go from the sublime to the ridiculous. He once had the Glamorgan fielders in hysterics when he came lunging forward to see off a delivery from Robert Croft and split open the back of his trousers, treating wicket-keeper Adrian Shaw to a fuller than expected view of the crease. Oooh I did like that one Crofty!

While it can be amusing one minute, first-class cricket, despite its often genteel environs, is a genuinely dangerous game. As a 'keeper, you're certainly more in the line of fire than most and hardly a season went by without the sickening crack of an exocet from Martin McCague or Alan Igglesden clunking you straight on the nose. Generally however I was pretty lucky. The worst incident came in 1987 when we were playing Lancashire at Liverpool. Derek Underwood was bowling when the Lancs opener David Varey came forward, bat and pad together, and the ball reared up viciously after glancing the pad and hit me flush in the eye. It was pretty painful for thirty seconds, but I brushed myself down and got on with the game. As we were in Liverpool, it was refusing to "calm down" and after a couple more rather sore overs I found I had a black spot in my eye. I was advised by the guys that I'd better leave the field and tests at the ophthalmic hospital later showed that I'd flattened my retina and had bleeding in the back of the eye. The retina wasn't an issue, but, because of the bleeding, I wasn't supposed to run, skip or jump or listen to music any more raucous than Mantovani for three weeks. It was reasonable advice because if it bled again, there was a very real possibility of blindness in that eye. After the three weeks had elapsed, I was given a clean bill of health and could resume my career.

Unfortunately for Middlesex and former Kent 'keeper, Paul Downton, luck was definitely not on his side. It was nothing to do with the wicket but when the ball hit the stumps, the bail flicked off and hit him straight in the eye. Such was the damage to the cornea that it finished his career. That cruel million-to-one chance just illustrates what a dangerously fine line all cricketers can walk.

Despite these threats to life and limb, I never wanted to follow Australian Ian Healy's lead and keep in a helmet. The restriction on vision and mobility was too high a price to pay. That said, the area of the wicket you most had to be wary of was the rough outside the right-hander's leg stump, known as "the jungle". A good left-arm spinner can cause mayhem if he can regularly plant it in "Injun country" - it can go sideways, climb, trundle along the deck, you name it.

Helmets, or "lids" as they are often known, don't guarantee one hundred per cent protection. In 1988, Chris Penn was bowling extremely sharply in the last championship game and was charging in towards Surrey's Ian Greig. Although Greig was wearing a full-face helmet the ball still managed to squeeze in above the visor and pole-axe him. He was gashed badly above the eye, although I'm sure his psychological injuries stayed with him a long time after the stitches were removed. On other days lids can be life savers. The closest I ever came to seeing a player losing his life on a cricket field was at Lord's when Martin McCague struck Middlesex's John Carr. It was a quick, bouncy wicket and Macca was bounding in like an Irish Wolfhound on acid. Carr took a big lunge forward to defend a good length ball which then unexpectedly reared up from nowhere. He wasn't wearing a visor and time seemed to stand still as everyone close to the bat anticipated with horror the likely outcome of Carr's terrible misfortune. On impact his head flew back with a sickening whiplash and for a second or two we all feared the worst. It then turned out that the eighty miles per hour delivery had actually hit him squarely on the peak of the helmet. The ball might have been smiling but Carr certainly wasn't. An inch lower and I'm convinced it would have been fatal.

"Form", that most transient of phenomena, is something that deserts most players at least once a season and I was no exception. Cricket's played mostly in the mind and while you need to have the necessary ability to start with, everything then revolves around channelling your own mental attitude. Your biggest opponent in any game is yourself. It's all very well trying to outwit eleven guys from another county, but if you're not in tune with your own state of mind, you might as well leave your coffin in the boot of the car.

Batsmen who believe they can pull themselves out of a lean spell by taking up residence in the nets are largely kidding themselves. With the pressure off, anyone can look a million dollars. But it's what happens in the middle that counts. If I was going through a bad patch with the bat, I'd walk out to the crease making every effort to talk myself into a positive frame of mind. I told myself to show self-confidence in my body language, keep loose and watch the ball onto the bat. As long as I could remain focused on these three key objectives, the runs should naturally start to flow again.

Wicket-keeping was exactly the same. For no apparent reason

some days I'd lose the ability to glove a ball cleanly. I'd be cowering behind the stumps praying that the batsman would hit the ball so my ineptitude would not be exposed. In combating the spectre of negativity I'd discipline myself to step back, take stock and replay the basics over and over in my head. Was I watching the ball all the way into my gloves? Were my hands soft enough?

Standing back, you're nothing more than a glorified goal-keeper and your mobility is compromised if you're too tense. One of the ways I used to relax myself was to sing Chris Eubank's *Simply the Best* anthem under my breath. I must have looked pretty much like Tina Turner coming to the wicket after some of my heavier nights, so I suppose it was appropriate at least in one respect!

Life can be difficult enough out in the middle, but sometimes you've got to also contend with the men in the white coats. As counties, you occasionally come up against umpires that seem, for some unknown reason, to have something against you. Despite the fact that most of the English umpires' panel was of the highest quality, the performances of one or two continually failed to pass muster. In my time the name that would trigger the loudest moans in the Kent dressing-room was that of Alan Whitehead. A good umpire, like an official in any sport, should go about his business almost unnoticed. To me, Whitehead, in his officious and brusque manner, appeared to want the game to revolve around him at all times.

Typical of my relationship with him was an incident in a vital Sunday League game against Somerset at Taunton in 1997. It was developing into a very close tussle that was looking to go either way when we had to come off due to rain. We were batting second and we were slightly behind the rate on Duckworth-Lewis, so an abandonment and two points each at a crucial stage of the season was a comprimise we would have definitely settled for. To my consternation we were informed that we were to go back out, despite the fact that it was still drizzling. So I went to the umpires' room and asked why, if you don't start a game in the rain, we were nevertheless expected to brave the elements. I recieved rather short shrift: 'I've said we're going back out, and we're going back out'. So back out we went and I decided I'd save my thoughts on the matter for my captain's report.

As the match progressed we lost a couple of wickets and I went out to bat. Whitehead gestured abruptly at me as I asked for a guard and, when I took a single to join him at the non-striker's end, he said he wanted to see me in his office afterwards. After the game, which incidentally we won, I made my way to the headmaster's study to find myself on the receiving end of a tirade of puffed-up self-importance:

'Don't ever do that to me again and question my decision in front of sponsors! I don't like people who undermine me and if you want to do so, we can sort it out somewhere else!'

Though it was awfully tempting to stick his light meter somewhere where the sun was guaranteed not to shine, I didn't want to become embroiled in an unnecessary melodrama and simply said:

'Alan, I've come up here to sort this out like two adults and look at the way you're behaving', and left him to it.

I also believe that Whitehead's attitude was a key factor when Martin McCague lost his action and suffered a serious case of the "yips" for a season. Macca was really struggling with his run-up in the championship match the previous day and had been warned for a second, albeit unintentional, bouncer in an over. A third bouncer would mean he'd have to be taken off and wouldn't be allowed to bowl again in the innings, so I told him to cut down his run-up to three or four paces and just try and see the over out. Unfortunately it didn't work and he bowled a very slow beamer at Rob Turner. Now any umpire with an ounce of reason or compassion would have been able to understand the situation and show a bit of lenient common sense. Not Alan Whitehead. His usual domineering overzealousness in stopping him bowling compounded Martin's loss of confidence and we basically lost our principal strike bowler for a season.

Some umpires, like Dickie Bird, were a joy to play with. Whatever his failings, you always knew what you got with Dickie and, most importantly, he was consistent. As a batsman, if you were on the front foot, you were safe. He's a lovely guy who would always help players and was far more astute and rational than the somewhat eccentric image that he'd like to project.

Most county cricketers have their favourite Dickie Bird story and mine underlines the humanity, although some would say scattiness, of the man. In 1993, Graham Cowdrey and I were batting against Northamptonshire at Canterbury when Curtly Ambrose bowled a rising leg-side delivery to Graham that flicked something on the way through. Whether it was glove, arm, chest or nipple, I couldn't tell. There was a big appeal from the 'keeper and slips and Curtly followed through with his arm in air to signal to the scorers to chalk him up another one on the board. But Graham just stood there. Dickie did his "That's owwwwt" party piece and Graham eventually dragged himself towards the pavilion in disgust, rubbing his arm. We both knew that the younger Cowdrey wasn't the sort of player to try it on so Dickie turned to me, his face riddled with apprehension.

'Eee, Marshy, Cowdrey's roobin' 'is arm! I don't know what to do!'

'I think you've made a mistake,' I replied, seizing the chance to exploit his better nature, 'Call him back!'

By this time, Graham was half-way back to the pavilion and Dickie was shouting 'Cow, Cow, coom back, coom back!' With Graham stopping and then starting and half turning round, it looked to the guys on our balcony that he was indulging in a bit of verbal fisticuffs with the Yorkshire official. Daryl Foster was shouting 'Graham, flamin' well come off' and Dickie was hollering 'Coom back, coom back', so with all the to and fro it was all starting to resemble *Kramer versus Kramer* in flannels. With Graham back at the crease like a dog returneth to his vomit, the Northants players were naturally incensed that he'd been granted a stay of execution merely because he whinged. Their skipper, Allan Lamb, could perhaps have been excused for giving Dickie the lambasting he did.

'Fuck's sake Dickie,' he screeched in a tone of shrillness similar to a strimmer suffering a power surge, 'you gave him out, so he's out!'

After several minutes' furore it all died down again, although it riled Curtly enough for him to step up about three gears.

Dickie took a fair bit of stick in the press over his shilly-shallying that day, so much so that he even threatened the *Daily Telegraph* scribe Charles Randall with legal action!

On the cricket field, I rarely courted controversy over the course of my career. I had to wait until 1999, my last full season in the first team, for my on-field behaviour to come under scrutiny. We were playing Sussex in the championship when I couldn't help noticing that Michael di Venuto (which I'd previously assumed was a flavour of ice cream) was standing a mile out of his crease when facing Mark Ealham. Frustrated that he was giving himself too much of an advantage, I concocted a plan with Ealy whereby on a certain ball in the over I would sprint up stealthily to the wicket and try and stump him off a slow, leg-side widish one. Although the ploy worked and he was comfortably out of his ground as I whipped off the bails, the umpire, Pasty Harris, was away with the fairies and missed what was going on. He didn't uphold the appeal.

A couple of months later, Essex's Ronnie Irani had virtually set up camp at the wicket and was playing a similar game to di Venuto. I was starting to get a little tired of the constant shuffling back and forth, so I reconvened with Ealy with a view to repeating our little stunt. By coincidence, Pasty Harris was again the square leg umpire, so I instructed Macca to stand next to him and subtly alert him to the situation. At the given moment I skipped up to the wicket, scooped up the ball and broke the stumps. Ronnie, who was way out of his crease turned around knowing full well that he'd been suckered. 'Oh no Marshy, you bastard!' he huffed as he prepared to make his way to the pavilion. Having this time seen everything unfold, Pasty then conferred with his colleague, Trevor Jesty, and between them they turned down the appeal, invoking laws 42.2 and 42.3 on "ungentlemanly conduct".

Ronnie actually saw the funny side and later congratulated me on a "top effort", but from the general furore and gnashing of teeth in the national press you'd have thought I'd just head-butted the Queen Mother. In any event, I'd highlighted a grey area in the laws which was clarified in time for the next season. Nice to know I've been of some use!

SEVEN

Bettin' and Boozin'

Professional cricket ranks alongside on-site security and lighthouse-keeping as one of those occupations where the ability to kill time should be an integral part of the job description. On rainy days when there was no real likelihood of there being any play, the atmosphere in the pavilion could resemble one of those POW huts in a John Mills Sunday afternoon matinée. As we couldn't dig our way out, idle hands often found their way to a deck of cards. We were certainly never short of spades!

It's one of life's unwritten laws. If you leave a group of bored young sportsmen together for any length of time, it is inevitable that some moral weakling is going to suggest a wager. At Kent, there was a degenerate gambling sub-committee that consisted of me, Mark Benson and Chris and Graham Cowdrey. We all probably ended up with considerable deficits on our gambling accounts over the years, and while on occasions it admittedly did get very silly, I can't say any of us really regretted our indiscretions. Apart from perhaps the South African Roy Pienaar.

We were playing down in Folkestone and the day's cricket was rained off fairly early so Chris Cowdrey invited some of the regulars back to his place for a card school. One of the party was Mr Pienaar, who was only a very occasional gambler. Roy was our overseas player at the time and, as he'd only been over a little while, the club was still paying him in cash. As it often does on rainy, windswept

123

afternoons, it started to turn into a bit of a session and after only fifty minutes of stud poker, Roy had lost his entire salary of £1,500, most of it to the host's Cincinnati Kid-brother, Graham!

Things gradually calmed down after that because from a psychological point of view, it's difficult to go out to bat with a clear mind if you're fretting about the month's wages you've just lost to some unscrupulous dressing-room shark. Big money stakes could also fuel animosity between players and the management sensibly put an end to our high rolling mid-match interludes.

It certainly didn't discourage our own little syndicate however. Yet even among the hard core, it became pretty evident that "honour" was at a premium. We were once playing at that most salubrious of cricket grounds, Ilford, when Mark Benson asked me as I was padding up, who I fancied to win out of the French and the All Blacks in the in the rugby world cup. I said I thought New Zealand would absolutely murder France, so he asked me what odds I'd offer him for a French victory. The speed at which he snapped up my offer of three to one was in hindsight suspiciously enthusiastic, but at the time I thought nothing of it and went out to bat already mentally spending my £50 banker. Not long afterwards I was trudging back to the dressing-room having been bowled all ends up by Neil Foster for not very many and gazed up at the score on the telly in the hope of some solace from a Froggie trouncing. But to add insult to injury, the treacherous French were winning the game with one minute to go! France duly held on and I was sitting there completely stuffed with no runs to my name, owing Benny £150!

It wasn't until about an hour afterwards that one of the guys came up to ask me whether I'd been stupid enough to have a bet with Mark on the rugby.

'You silly bastard', he chortled, 'they played that game last night. You were watching a recording!'

That bugger Benson knew the result before he offered me the bet. And he would have kept the money too!

Mark and I always had a running account going between us.

Sometimes, though, we'd join forces and have punt on a few outrageous accumulators. Over the years we must have got through more yankees than Sitting Bull at the Little Bighorn! In 1989 one of our more fanciful bets actually looked like it was going to come in and reward us all handsomely. Mark, Graham and I had placed very similar accumulators on major sporting events over the course of three months and all of the three bets were now hanging on the final leg, the winner of the Football League Championship. I remember we were all licking our chops in eager anticipation as we drove down from Trent Bridge to watch the championship decider between Liverpool and Arsenal, live and exclusive on ITV. If the Scousers could avoid defeat by two clear goals and thereby clinch the title, each of us would be better off to the tune of between two and three thousand pounds.

In this situation, true gambling professionals would have assessed the situation and laid the bet off to ensure a decent return, however the game finished. Arsenal were a thumping 8/1 to win the title that morning, so it would have been very straightforward to buy ourselves a little insurance. Unfortunately we got greedy and decided, like every other sane sports fan in the country save the most rabid Gooner, that the scenario of the Arse winning two-nil at Anfield was simply not going to happen. Despite Alan Smith's opener it was still not going to happen as the clock ticked over into stoppage time. Then John Barnes lost concentration and in a very un-isotonic moment stabbed a weak shot into Seaman's arms instead of taking the sensible option of shielding the ball in the corner. The Arsenal goalie, thankfully then in his pre-pony tail days, proceeded to hoof the ball hopefully up field, Michael Thomas latched onto it and, whoops, it's two bloody nil! As Brian Moore went barmy I felt sure Mark was going to put his head through the telly.

County cricketers can clock up inter-galactic mileage travelling up and down the country over the course of a season and a little gamble was a fun way to combat the tedium of the motorway slog. Tearing around from ground to ground with my regular co-pilot

Benny, a mobile phone and a copy of the *Racing Post* were essential pieces of kit. In our heyday, when Mark and I would bet on two flies crawling up a wall, we used to play a silly little game called "A Round of Golf". Each of us would nominate a car that was at least a couple of hundred yards ahead and our "score" would be determined by the aggregate of the three numbers on the number plate. Having nominated, I'd then ignite the after-burners and we'd hare off after the target vehicle so we could read the figures. With each car having three digits, a round consisted of six cars with the lower score winning. At five pound a point, I only had to be trailing Sergeant Bilko by twenty "shots" and I'd be getting out of the motor owing him £100!

In the early days I was a pretty heavy punter, that was until the day I got my fingers badly burnt by the curse of all degenerate gamblers: "the sure thing". It was the first Sunday League game of the season and Graham Cowdrey and I were travelling down to Worcester and we thought en route we'd take in some equestrian activity at Newbury on the Saturday. As we all know, a little knowledge is a dangerous thing and we approached the afternoon's card with all the bravado of punters who reckoned they were one step ahead of the market. With Graham being on friendly terms with more racing big-wigs than the Queen, we'd occasionally be privy to some supposedly top grade info. We knew that our old pals, the top trainer/jockey combo Michael Stoute and Walter Swinburn, would be in action that day, so we called the stable and made a few subtle enquiries as to the form.

Our contact at the stable couldn't have been more bullish. She was convinced that in the third race, the John Porter Stakes, Michael's horse, Rock Hopper, was very definitely the class of the field and would stroll it. All through the week we'd therefore been on the 'phone, checking the horse's progress on the gallops and ensuring his hay was being served to him at the correct temperature. All seemed to be going fine until the Thursday when the stable lad reported that he'd looked a little flat and seemed to be lacking the sparkle that would have otherwise made him the day's banker bet. If we'd backed the horse on the basis of this information and it had lost, we would have looked like prize schmucks, so we took what we thought was the prudent decision to switch our entire wager onto the second favourite instead. Typically, Rock Hopper then proceeded to absolutely obliterate the field to win by a country mile and take £500 of our money with him. I would like to have personally hopped on the rocks of that stable lad at that particular moment. Not a good start.

Well, we took the view that our information was essentially sound and it was just a case that we weren't quite interpreting it correctly. According to our oracle back at the Stoute camp, the weekend's other certainty was a runner at Ayr called Polish King. As it was allegedly their prospective Derby entry for the following year we decided to keep the faith. I made my way over to the track-side William Hill and, noting that this apparent certainty was attractively priced favourite at 6/4, I placed £500 on the nose. Intriguingly it drifted out then to 7/4 and when it then ticked over another notch to 2/1, I grabbed my opportunity to make some hay and thumped down another £300 to make it the biggest bet of my life. Michael Stoute's Derby entry in a six horse race! How could it fail? I can only think that he must have meant donkey derby as the recalcitrant nag limped home a pathetic fourth.

When you've suffered that much pain, you might as well be hung for a sheep as a lamb, so I closed my eyes and slapped £50 on the 7/1 shot Lahib in the last race of the day, a cavalry charge for maidens. Despite leading all the way it got pipped on line by a short head. It was the last bet I placed for some considerable time!

In 1995 I took my indulgence in the sport of kings a stage further by becoming an owner! Lady Herries, Graham Cowdrey's step-mother, runs a stable and our syndicate of nine (which included Jazzer, Macca, Iggy and former Gillingham chairman Bernie Baker) speculated £2,000 on the purchase of a backward two-year-old filly. Aravinda, as we decided to name her, was still rather small, so we waited until she was a three-year-old before running her for the first time. If she ran as quickly as she ate, I'm sure we'd have had a potential classic winner on our hands. The moment of truth came in a maidens' race at an evening meeting at Epsom. They were out of the stalls at half past seven and she came trailing in at a quarter past eight - last!

'Oi tink she was pickin' op at bit at t'end' was the only consolation our jockey could offer us. Given the inordinate amount of time it had taken him to negotiate her home, I'm surprised he didn't ask us for overtime.

Any illusions that Aravinda could have just been having an off day were categorically dispelled a few weeks later when she did exactly the same thing at Windsor. Having injured herself slightly, though I hasten to add not through excessive speed, this born loser was gracefully retired after a mere two races. Spared the glue factory after an eleventh hour reprieve, Aravinda was last seen eating Bernie Baker's wife out of house and home at her stables in Grafty Green. Never again.

Trevor Ward's old friend Peter O'Toole's assumption that cricketers these days only seem to be interested in getting pissed was uncomfortably near the mark for some players. Some blokes just didn't know when to stop! The drinker for whom I had the greatest respect was undoubtedly the former Kent top order batsman, Derek Aslett. Now Derek's not a large bloke, in fact he's not a million miles away from what some people would term "scrawny". You won't, however, meet anyone who can sink pints of beer like he does. He's one of these freaks of nature who can open their gullet in such a way that they can consume copious amounts of liquid without the need to swallow. Beers just go straight down, one after another.

When a dozen or more cricketers meet in the bar, stalking horses like Derek are gold dust. What made him extra special was that his diminutive stature meant nobody would ever take him seriously as a swiller extraordinaire. So with Derek practically unbeatable, I suggested it was high time we rolled him out into the beer drinking circuit, organised a sting and made ourselves a bit of money. And I was going to be his manager!

Our first opportunity was to come at Worcester and our victim was to be one I.T. Botham. Beefy had always been a great believer in his own publicity when it came to drinking and he'd never refuse to pick up a gauntlet that in any way challenged his machismo. He was the perfect target for a hustle.

Now the two teams were socialising in a hospitality tent after the day's play and I had already briefed Derek to stand around looking insipid while the rest us tried to tee up Botham by dragging the conversation around to boozing. When the topic finally arose I made my play.

'Cor, I tell you what Beefy, if you want to talk about drink, you want to talk to Derek over there. Now he *can* drink!'

Botham didn't just swallow the bait hook, line and sinker, he bit off half the rod as well. 'What?!' he guffawed, 'That little ginger-headed four-eyed twat over there? You're having a laugh.'

I smelled blood. 'No, honestly Beefy. I reckon he could take you on, I really do.'

'Well I'm going to have some of that,' piped the greatest ever all-rounder, 'let's get it on!'

Trying not to dribble too much in anticipation I was careful to add a rider.

'My man's a professional, he doesn't do anything for nothing you know!'

The "kerching" of cash registers started to go off wildly in my mind when Botham tapped his wallet in his back pocket and promised in a tone as smug as you will ever hear, 'However much you want, sunshine.'

So the challenge was on. It would take place in the Worcester dressing-room after the next day's play and the winner would be the first to down a pint of bitter on a best of three basis. We got all the Kent boys together and raised a nice little pot of £350, while Botham, in a fit of cock-sure complacency you wouldn't even have credited to a fox with a duplicate key to the hen house, decided to stump up Worcester's money all on his own.

All twenty-two players crammed into the dressing-room and, on the referee's whistle, the gulping commenced. Our man did not disappoint. In round one, Derek must have done it in two and a half seconds flat, leaving Botham with just under half a pint left. In the second round, Derek supped up in about two seconds and Botham didn't even get below half way. The poor legend was stuffed out of sight two-nil. Give him his due though, he reached for his cheque book and straight away wrote out a kite for £350. 'There you are boys,' he cheerfully conceded, 'I've been done!'

My days of being Derek Aslett's drinking pimp didn't last long as word got round pretty quick. A couple of weeks later we did manage to relieve Northamptonshire of £200 when we saw off Geoff Cook, their previously undefeated, undisputed champion, but after that most counties had pretty much wised up. Fun while it lasted though!

It's a lucky thing that Derek didn't come with us on Martin McCague's stag weekend as we all would have been totally wasted trying to keep up with him. Being best man, it was up to me to get everything organised for our trip to the Emerald Isle to watch the Ireland-France rugby game. I couldn't get hold of the tickets, but I at least managed sort out the flights and accommodation, trusting to luck that somewhere I'd able to find eighteen rugby tickets all in a row. We were leaving from Stansted on the Friday lunchtime and were returning on the Sunday in the late afternoon. The one rule of the weekend's obligatory booze orgy of a competition was that in the intervening forty-eight hours, only one tipple was permitted to pass our lips: Guinness.

On arrival we made our way to the Old Wesley's ground to watch the 'B' international to see if we could pick up some tickets for

Saturday's match. We were progressing neatly into our fourth or fifth pint when Macca announced that, in an attempt to pre-empt the inevitable ritual humiliation that by tradition all impending grooms must suffer, he was going to perform his own forfeit. The clubhouse was a rather olde worlde affair and Martin explained to the assembled throng that he would mimic the local custom by stripping stark naked and climbing up onto some wood-worm ridden rafters, some twelve feet above the floor, and then throwing himself down into our linked arms below. When he gets up a head of steam, you don't get in the big lad's way, so we all steadied ourselves as the seventeen-and-a-half stone block of Ulster gristle edged along the beam. Without any clothes on, he needed to be careful as one slip and he could have easily ended up leaving his wedding equipment behind, dangling on a rusty nail! Egged on by the chants of the regulars he jumped off in a swallow-dive before the twelve of us had time to properly link arms. We only managed to partially break his fall and Macca ended up hitting the deck with such a thump that we thought he'd killed himself! To have the groom die on us four hours into the stag weekend would not have been the optimum start, so we all breathed a hefty sigh of relief when he eventually picked himself up, removed specks of saw-dust from his bodily hair, told us we were useless bastards and went off to look for his Guinness.

We managed to get into the full international the next day after I'd got us tickets by chasing a compliant touch judge up and down the line in a morning match, so by the Sunday all that was left to us was the competition. Luckily a couple of the boys had found a very amenable Dublin publican who let us in before time and even poured us up a round of Guinnesses on the house while we waited for him to open. We'd obviously found the perfect venue for the showdown and decided to stay there the until it was time to leave for the airport. The contest was hotting up nicely. Macca had drunk about seventy pints, which was a hell of an effort, although there was another mate of ours, Don Smart, who was handily placed just behind him on sixty-three. By the time we had reached the airport bar just after one, Macca decided that enough was enough and he was going to stick, or perhaps that should be 'sick', on seventy-four. Don was only about five behind now and one last run up the rails might just be enough to see him home, so we looked on in admiration as he calmly knocked yet another one back. Having convinced himself of his own invincibility, he announced he would do the same again, and in the space of five minutes, he'd notched up another four to put himself only two behind the leader. With his bladder screaming for mercy, Don sidled off to jet wash a urinal. That was the last we saw of him as he passed out in his Irish bog and ended up missing the plane! All those who slipped off the pace were always left to crash and burn. Those were the rules of the game. For what is was worth, and it was only really kudos, Macca took the prize having pipped Don by three pints. For the record, I languished way back in ninth place having supped a next-to-worthless fifty-four.

With the fun and games over, we waited in the check-in queue, bleary-eyed and reeking of stout. Standing behind about twenty people in such a dishevelled state was becoming a little tedious, so I decided a short-cut was in order. I went up, put my bag on the conveyor belt, climbed aboard and followed it through. There I was, face down, following my bag through the X-ray machine like Superman. Of course, I thought this was most amusing but, having reached the other side, the security guard had different ideas as he pinned me into a corner.

'Are you fockin' stupid or what?', he growled in a tone of voice you rarely hear on the adverts.

Mischievously I replied, 'Yes, I do believe I *am* stupid.'

'If oi were you', he went on, 'oi'd go straight back and see a ducta'.

In another unwise attempt at humour I said, 'Well, who's been telling you what I've been getting up to then?'

He eyes betrayed no glint of amusement and for a horrible moment I thought I was to be stranded as well, but he eventually

took his hands off my jacket after I confessed to being a naughty boy and I high-tailed it onto the plane.

Someone else who can drink like a fish is my old mucker Robin Smith. I linked up with him for the first time in the winter of 1986/87 when we were invited to join a touring party of English professionals to play Barbados in three one-day internationals. Very soon it became patently clear that we were both singing from the same hymn sheet and we decided to embark on a marathon binge of excess. When it was all over, we calculated that over the three week tour, we got in no more than thirty hours' kip which, if you average it out, is not a lot.

Most of the extra-curricular activity took place at a club in Bridgetown called The Warehouse. From there one night a chain of events would unravel that would lead to the centre of the island's capital being plunged into gridlock. Every time we went there we would be greeted by a charming Rastafarian who would flash us a goofy smile and say 'Look after your car boss?' Being familiar with this kind of public spritedness after trips to the odd northern football ground, we'd tip him a couple of dollars and all would be well. It was however obvious that he was just taking the money and disappearing off to his local ganga emporium, so after a week of this nightly rigmarole we told him we'd prefer to take the risk of making do without his security consultancy service. Oblivious to his cries of 'Hey, man, you never know what might happen!' we strode nonchalantly into the club like a couple of Oliver Tobiases. We should have known better.

When we eventually came back, the car, a little Mini Moke, was still in situ and all looked well. But when I got in and turned the key, nothing happened. Not even the starter motor was turning over so we obviously had a bit of a problem. We were both to car maintenance what Cyril Smith was to hang-gliding but we duly opened up the bonnet for a prod and twist. Neither of us knew what the hell we were looking for but after ten minutes of clueless fiddling Robin said, 'Hang on a minute Marshy, can you see a battery?' The giveaway rectangular hole where the battery should have been meant that we had indeed been done by the cheeky Rasta and were now, at four in the morning, well and truly stuck.

Anybody who's had a car for more than five minutes will tell you that you can't bump start a car without a battery, but we had a go anyway. For some reason we kept pushing the lifeless vehicle into the centre of town and eventually we came to the single track bridge after which the capital is named. I still don't quite know what our motivation was but we decided to push the Moke to the brow of the deserted bridge and leave it. We took a hike for half a mile, got a taxi back to our digs and thought no more of it.

The next morning we were on the beach and the police arrived. We hadn't remembered that the Moke was registered in our names and they were naturally interested to find the people who had caused, so they said, the town's worst traffic jam for several years. There were, apparently, half-mile tail backs either end of the bridge! With a bit of nimble thinking I suggested that we'd left it because we were too drunk to drive and that some unscrupulous locals must had taken it for a prank. So we were pretty lucky to get away with it and only dared talk about our night as international traffic terrorists once we'd got on the plane back to England.

It may have got us into a bit of trouble that night but earlier in the tour that little car could well have saved our lives! Another one of our haunts was a club called Harbour Lights and one night, after a relatively restrained 2.30am finish, we thought we'd drive over and take advantage of Bridgetown's all-night fast-food boulevard, Baxter Street, and pick ourselves up something typically tropical and chips. As we got in the Moke, we noticed a local guy thumbing a lift. As he said he only wanted to be dropped just round the back of Baxter Street we invited him to hop in. Innocents abroad or what! We went past our destination, took a left, then a right and then another right and all of a sudden we found ourselves in the "cheaper" end of town. After he directed us down a dark dead-end street with a row of garages at the end we were starting to feel more than a little uncomfortable and when a posse of five motorcyclists swung out to follow us, the awful realisation dawned that we were being set up. Robin's got South African national service under his belt and swiftly booted out our passenger and swung the Moke around for the getaway. As we hared back out of the alley, the bikers were now in hot pursuit and we were making ready to defend ourselves with a couple of empty Banks' beer bottles. As the first set of traffic lights were red and there was no way through, we clutched our weapons and prayed that it paid to drink and drive. Then, just as the bikers loomed large in the rear-view mirror and our tickers had accelerated to warp factor fifteen, the lights mercifully changed and we melted away into the darkness.

All that for a flying fish roll!

EIGHT

Supporters and Detractors

The wonderful supporters of Kent County Cricket Club have deserved much better than the starvation rations they've been served up over the last twenty-plus years. Knowledgeable and fiercely partisan, they have stuck with their side through two pretty lean decades, showing levels of endurance through adversity that even Ernest Shackleton would have craved.

On a personal level, the rapport enjoyed with the supporters was vital in keeping me with the county on the two or three occasions through my career when I felt events were conspiring to force me to ply my trade elsewhere. The flood of letters of support from members when I lost the captaincy or when Paul Nixon joined the staff made me realise how much respect the Kent fans had for me and fired my resolve to meet the challenges head-on.

Following county cricket is a passion for a lot of people and there are of course certain members for whom the fortunes of the club are the be all and end all of life itself. On occasions you have to steel yourself as a player to remember that the supporters pay your wages and you have to let them have their say, however misinformed they may appear. There was the occasional zealot who made it his life's mission to question and criticise the Kent captain for every decision he made. One particular character I remember was "Anonymous" of Folkestone, no doubt the illegitimate fruit of some seedy seaside indiscretion on the part of "Disgusted" of Tunbridge Wells. When we were captains, Chris Cowdrey, Mark Benson and I were forever getting letters from this guy telling us that every toss decision, bowling change and field placing was a disgrace and that we should resign immediately! These letters generally came in at one a week and we'd pass them around the dressing-room, laugh at them and then place them neatly in the bin.

As more razzmatazz has entered the game, the profile of cricketing public has gradually changed over the years too. The atmosphere generated at a day-night match can be as vibrant and electric as a championship game can be bland and uninspired. The mood of the crowd for a match under lights can give you the adrenaline rush that is simply not there in other forms of cricket. The traditionalists may hate it, but I love the spectacle, the noise and the crowd involvement of a one-day game.

The boisterousness of certain crowds can produce some very funny moments. Yorkshire crowds are as droll as they are vociferous and I remember one amusing incident when were playing up at Scarborough in a one-day game involving Matthew Walker. Now for those who can't picture him, Matthew, also known as Pumba (the squat little hog in *The Lion King*), definitely wouldn't worry too many people in an arse kicking competition. On this particular occasion Matthew was coming on to bowl and, from the cheap seats, this booming Yorkshire voice piped up 'Hi-hoh!', and then another four joined in with a chorus of 'Hi-hoh, hi-hoh, it's off to work we go'. Walks could barely keep his composure as he ran up to the wicket and only just managed to release the ball. The batsman, Michael Vaughan, and I were in such hysterics that if the delivery had been straight, neither of us would have been anywhere near it!

When we were playing at home we had the luxury of a set of supporters whose fervour was only matched by that of the Roses counties. Teams hated coming to Kent because the home crowd's complete lack of sporting impartiality created an atmosphere most of them were totally unused to. And there's nothing wrong with that. Your home ground should be your fortress, so what do you gain from clapping *their* boundaries or *their* wickets?

The Lancy-Lancy-Lancy-Lancy Lancashire supporters are also a pretty colourful bunch but occasionally, like all crowds, they can take their partisanship one step too far. We were playing a one-day game at Old Trafford and I remember Richard Ellison sliding for a ball close to the boundary rope. The grass was very greasy and as Richard slid, he got his arm caught below his body and was unable to protect himself as he hurtled towards a wrought iron bench. He ended up hitting the side of it with the bridge of his nose and there was enough AB negative gushing everywhere to make even Sam Peckinpah wince. As we ran over to attend to him, one Lancy spectator shouted out generously, 'Get oop you soft southern bastard'. Incensed, three of us went over to confront them and beckoned the perpetrator of this fairly sick comment, in rather Anglo-Saxon terms, to come forward and identify himself. Unfortunately it appeared he was a little bit soft too.

When you consider the number of balls that go flying into the crowd, it is amazing that more people don't get hit. Granted that in championship games the attendances were so small that we could have stood there hitting sixes all day and never land one within twenty yards of a paying punter but, by the same token, when the ground was full, balls used to fly in and miraculously manage to just miss both cars and spectators. In mid-afternoon, after a few beers, you used to see the old boys in the front row in their deck chairs, deep in the land of nod. Once in a while some bullet of a half-volley would be dispatched across the outfield, skip up off the boundary rope and arrow towards an aged member's cranium. From the middle you'd clench your buttocks and think to yourself 'Christ, they're dead!' but somehow at the last millisecond they'd tilt their head and the ball would skim past their ear as they snored away oblivious. Some of them never knew how close they were to not waking up at all!

My excellent relationship with the media was similar to that I enjoyed with the Kent members, especially in my first couple of seasons in the mid-eighties. Then the *Kent Messenger's* James Allen came along and from day one he seemed to manage to get a snide dig in at me no matter how well I performed. His penchant for damnation through faint praise was typified by his summation of my 1990 season: 'While it would be hard to make a case for him being the most accomplished wicket-keeper on the county circuit, his contributions with the bat - he fell just 89 short of 1,000 runs last summer - have generally offset any short-comings.' Whether this lukewarm attitude was out of a personal dislike of me or of the way I played cricket I don't know, but all it really served to do was to antagonise me into giving him fewer and fewer interviews. He didn't seem to understand that it's up to the local media to foster healthy working relationships with the county's cricket or football clubs so a mutually beneficial partnership can be developed. Like most things in life, it's a case of give and take.

In the second half of my career, Mark Pennell was the principal cricket writer for the *Kent Messenger* and I'm glad to say we've always had a good working relationship. It's not to say that he has never been critical of me, far from it. But what was conspicuously missing from his make-up was some hidden agenda to undermine either me or the club. He writes it as he sees it and I respect that. I know that some of the players are not all that keen on the way he reports but, for me, he's always been fair and I've always been happy to assist him wherever I could. The same goes for Radio Kent's Neil Bell and John Warnett who have been unstintingly positive and upbeat towards Kent cricket. Even if we've got our backs to the wall and the position is hopeless, they're still charged with a never say die spirit of optimism. For that reason alone, most of the guys on the staff are always happy to give them some waffle.

Outside the county, the provincial scribblers aren't always so generous. In that tight encounter at Lord's in 1997, the London *Evening Standard* bugled the headline in one of their early editions 'Ramprakash steers Middlesex to victory.' It must have come as a crushing blow to the tubes and buses full of exultant Middlesex fans who arrived home that evening to find that Kent had in fact won by four runs!

The fact that Kent, on the whole, enjoyed such rich support from members and media alike suggests that the principal reasons for our underachievement in the last twenty years must stem from within.

When it comes to rounding up the usual suspects, the Canterbury wicket can run, but it can't hide. The unpalatable fact of the matter is that it often gave us little or no assistance and therefore forfeited us the advantage of playing in front of such an excellent home crowd. The reason you play at home is to gain an edge over the opposition by tailoring the conditions to suit your strengths. Unfortunately at Kent, the ground staff seemed either unwilling or incapable of following our instructions and over the years we have missed out on that advantage.

In the early nineties we were fortunate enough to be able to field a skilled and varied attack that featured such classy spinners as Min Patel and Carl Hooper. Yet at Canterbury, Chris Cowdrey, Mark Benson and I were consistently thwarted by hideously green sons-of-pitches that could have been custom designed for our opponents' seam-based attacks. It was as if our groundsmen were trying to turn the St Lawrence into some sort of shrine to Alan Titchmarsh. It didn't matter that we couldn't win on it, just as long as it looked pretty. Go to other grounds and by September even test tracks like Old Trafford would resemble a Kansas dust bowl of the Great Depression. Come to Canterbury at the end of the season and you'd be greeted by the Garden of Eden.

In 1997 I told the *Kent Messenger* that if success was to return to Kent, it could only be achieved through a co-ordinated team effort from every element of the club, not just the players. On the playing side, we never felt we got the support we needed from either the ground staff or the administrators and we all ended up pulling in different directions. There was a paranoia about the club producing wickets that might attract the twitching noses of the pitch-inspectors, so these days the groundsman has carte blanche to prepare the pitch exactly as he sees fit. They didn't give us the tools so we couldn't finish the job.

The situation was no different at Maidstone. The groundsman, Malcolm Bristow, is so skilled and dedicated to his job that he used to produce wickets that would look as good after four days as they did on the first morning. A batting paradise was the last thing we wanted at The Mote because nine times out of ten we'd be playing lesser sides against whom we needed to get a result. Time and time again we'd have to sweat our nether regions off trying to force a result against the league's whipping boys. In 1996 we were playing Durham, who at the time were absolutely hopeless and were routinely getting rolled over in two days. We played right on the limit for the whole four days and only managed to scrape through for the win with ten overs remaining. It was almost as if you had to win a match twice sometimes at The Mote.

The best ground for us in terms of results was Tunbridge Wells because you'd always be guaranteed bounce and swing. Whether it was the flowering of the rhododendrons or the moistness of the atmosphere due to it being a spa town I don't know, but draws were a comparative rarity and we'd always manage to win more than we'd lose. It was exactly what a wicket should be: sporting and competitive. The bounce could occasionally get batsmen into trouble but, if you played well, you'd get full value for your shots. Its quick outfield meant that if you got in, you could score big runs.

Leaving the more cosmetic factors aside, the real reason that the county has underachieved over the last twenty years is that the committee has failed to move with the times. Cricket has progressed so much in the last few years but the administrators at Kent are still stuck with both feet in the past. Although there has been some change, the "Band of Brothers" influence is still all-pervasive. The real power brokers were "outsiders" like the dyed-in-the-wool traditionalist Jim Swanton who could wrap the committee round his little finger just by making a few 'phone calls.

As captain, I was frustrated by the "yes" men who sat on the committee merely for the prestige it offered. For them, it was all about status first and the good of the club second. Whenever a strong personality came along with a few fresh ideas, they very quickly closed ranks and endeavoured to force him out. The person I have in mind in this context is Jim Woodhouse, who was Chief Executive back in 1988. Jim was a very capable administrator who was also very positive towards the players. He was an excellent man manager who understood the players and what motivated them. Occasionally he'd take the unprecedented step of organising a team bonus if we had performed particularly well. We weren't exactly talking telephone numbers, but it was an important gesture that at last made us feel that we were being appreciated.

The new broom that Jim brought with him represented far too much of a threat to the old boys in their leather armchairs. So frightened were they that their comfortable, cosseted little world of self-interest would be upset, they marginalised him to such an extent that they made his position untenable. Basically, they ousted him to save their own hides.

County cricket clubs really need to leave behind the culture of jobs for the boys and committees for committees' sake. I sat on the cricket committee for two years as captain, and I quickly began to realise that I was there to keep a seat warm and little else. It all seemed so pointless. All the decisions we made could be over-turned by the general committee, so what was the point of us being there? We served about as much purpose as an ash tray on a motor bike.

The lesson of football has taught us that clubs need to be owned and run by businessmen who are sufficiently hard-nosed and unsentimental to grab it by the scruff of the neck and drag it into the twenty-first century. It's got to be said that the clerks at Kent were hardly supermen. You just have to look at Ken Bates at Chelsea. Not the world's most universally popular character, but he's had the acumen and sheer force of will to take a bankrupt and decrepit football club on the verge of an abyss to the status of arguably the country's most fashionable team. The way the situation is at the moment at Kent, it simply doesn't matter if the club does poorly. None of the executive committee members has any capital tied up in the club and therefore has no incentive to run it with flair, imagination and efficiency. Without the safety net of the ECB subsidies, the St Lawrence Ground would have been turned into an Asda superstore years ago.

There's so much that can be done to run Kent more professionally. It's been said for years that the marketing at the club is appalling. The club's monopoly of professional cricket in Kent has been played away with a dismal lack of imagination. Although I don't want to point the Bishop's Finger, I personally believe that the club undersold itself in its deal with the current main sponsor, Shepherd Neame. With the relative successes of 1997 suggesting that the club was at last on the up, the committee had a lot more scope for negotiation with big-hitting organisations. But then again, you just got the feeling that the partnership was a result of a comfortable arrangement, with committee members doing old pals a favour. If you'd had a top marketing specialist in charge, he probably wouldn't have touched the local brewery with a dung-infused barge pole. There are so many businesses out there who would love to support Kent County Cricket Club but can't because the club has left its sales and marketing machine stuck permanently in neutral. It has barely scratched the surface of the many lucrative opportunities that are out there.

The club also infuriates the playing staff with its ham-fisted handling of contracts and salaries. The committee are forever claiming that their hands are tied by poor revenues when it comes to salary negotiations. But if they're incompetent enough to generate only a subsistence level of income, why should the players have to pick up the tab? Players should be remunerated on the basis of individual and collective performances, not by how many gobstoppers they manage to shift in the confectionery stalls.

The playing staff is the Kent's best asset and most useful marketing tool, but the club shows no interest whatsoever when we suggest using our profiles to attract a bit of corporate interest over the winter months. Another sensible suggestion that fell on deaf ears involved getting more juniors along to Sunday League games. That's not saying that crowds of 7,000 are bad, but with a little effort they could be even better. In turn I told club secretaries Stuart Anderson and Paul Millman that the club should admit under twelves for nothing on a Sunday as the ground still has plenty of capacity and that each youngster would have to bring a least one adult with them. What you'd lose on letting in the few kids that regularly attend for nothing would be more than offset by the extra revenues generated by their parents' tickets and all the extra ice creams and other paraphernalia they'd be screaming for. What's more, the improved atmosphere would help the team play better and perhaps inspire a few of the newcomers into becoming regular supporters. In marketing terms it's an absolute no-brainer, but they wouldn't even entertain it on an experimental basis.

To be fair, this sort of administrative malaise is common to most counties. The only set-up that seems to want to look at things a little more progressively is Sussex. Tony Pigott managed to get a band together and oust the previous committee of laggards in a vote of no confidence and, with Dave Gilbert at the helm, the club adopted a far more forward-thinking agenda. With the help of major new sponsors they were able to be one of the first counties to bring in a big-money new signing in Chris Adams. I was captain when Chris came down with his agent to see us and I was desperate to sign him as he was a sparky, positive character who would be a great asset to our batting in both one-day and four-day cricket. But it fell through because Kent wouldn't get a sponsor and break the club's wage structure to pay for him. It's all very well having a pay structure, and players understand that. However, with home-grown talent thin on the ground, the time is coming when the top players are going to command far higher salaries and, if the county is not prepared to go out and find the necessary sponsorship to finance them, it will be left behind.

Kent need to get the right people in the right jobs and, although the signing of Paul Nixon was a step in the right direction, the club has to make this policy the rule rather than the exception. With the possible exclusion of David Masters, Kent haven't produced a home-grown fast bowler of any real repute in the last eight years. When you look at our batting, there doesn't seem to be anybody there who's capable of taking on the mantle of a Mark Benson or a Neil Taylor. With the talented Matthew Walker and David Fulton yet to perform to their full potential (although it's great to see that they have both made a blistering start to the current season), Kent will need to re-establish a tough, resilient core to its batting, and fast. The fact that we had to go out and offer a thirty-five-year-old Alan Wells a five year contract shows how fundamentally flawed the Kent system has become.

Ironically, when we were finally lucky enough to uncover a gem of a player in Paul Strang, the committee showed no enthusiasm whatsoever in keeping him on. Paul was the overseas player in my first full year as captain in 1997 and he was exactly the tonic Kent needed at the time. As well as being a top-class leg-spinner, he'd got a tremendous attitude and his exuberance and belief rubbed off on the rest of the team and helped pull through some of the weaker characters. His contribution was, without doubt, a major influence on our success that season.

With everything clicking on the field, I felt that at last we'd got the balance right. I therefore went to the committee and suggested that we extend Paul's contract for another season and pay off Carl Hooper. Carl, who was unavailable in 1997 because he was on tour with the West Indies, was a player of the highest calibre and you could never argue with his talent. But in many ways he was also a liability. As mentioned earlier, the main problem with Carl was his selfishness - he'd only perform for you when he felt like it and had little concept of teamwork. Although he was a nice guy, he was extremely unreliable and, some of the time, it was obvious he was just going through the motions. The committee, however, saw it differently and refused to pay Paul's wages on top of what it would cost to release Carl. So, for the sake of between £40,000 and £50,000, Kent could have secured themselves a player who could have taken the side to bigger and better things. Once again, the committee's blinkered attitude and fixation for collecting pound notes torpedoed common sense. Stuart Anderson's all-consuming preoccupation with being seen to be the Richard Branson of cricket club secretaries often infuriated me, especially in the context of his relative indifference to our fortunes on the field of play. In 1995 we were playing the West Indies in a sell-out three day game at Canterbury. Having made a dismal 95 in reply to the tourists' 337, it looked as if the game would be over before the final day. While the pace-men Gibson and Drakes went through us like a cheap curry in the first innings, the leg-spinner Dhanraj took centre stage in the second and had me and Mark Ealham stumped as we stumbled our way to a meagre advantage of 90. Despite having got out playing a totally legitimate shot, I nevertheless found myself curiously absent from Mr Anderson's good books.

The secretary was obviously smarting from the possibility of zero revenues from the third day and he marched up to Daryl Foster.

'I hope you're going to give Marsh an absolute bollocking!', he flapped, 'Does he not realise the we have full hospitality tomorrow in the marquees? This game better last. You tell your batsmen to stay there!'

Daryl was always on the players' side and found it all rather amusing, although when he came over to tell me about it, I found little reason to strap on my comedy corset. Next day in the treatment room I told some of the guys that, if Anderson dared to show his face, I'd be giving him the benefit of my full and frank opinion. Sure enough, ten minutes later, Anderson came in and I offered him the choice of a discussion there and then in front of the all and sundry or one-to-one out on the balcony. Noticing the flared profile of my nostrils, he wisely chose the al fresco option. I didn't beat about the bush.

'So, you're telling me how to play my cricket then are you? How I'm not supposed to come down the track and all that. Well I'll tell you I'd do exactly the same again. That's the way I play my cricket and I don't expect a secretary of a club to tell me how to play or how to bat. If it comes from my coach, then I'd listen to him. But I won't listen if it's some secretary who knows nothing about batting at all!'

Anyway, my little rant ended up with me asking for an apology. I could see he was turning mental cartwheels trying to save face and avoid owning up to his indiscretion but I was not going let him off the hook. Although he did eventually apologise, I doubt very much whether the underlying message had sunk in.

It's an episode that illustrates perfectly how hard the committee and the playing staff are pulling in different directions. The administrators of most county sides are little more than enthusiastic amateurs and, like all dabblers with pretensions beyond their abilities, regard any criticism, however constructively intentioned, with a mixture of scepticism and suspicion. If the Kent hierarchy cannot learn to overcome what is, in effect, its inferiority complex and incorporate the players in its decision making process, the club could well be doomed to underachieve for another twenty years.

Through its patronising attitude, the committee has made the players feel both inferior and excluded. It's time Kent became *one* cricket club.

NINE

Taking stock

In terms of players' professionalism, the game has definitely changed for the better in the last twenty years. When I first started, pre-season training consisted of little more than a few gentle morning fitness sessions at the University of Kent. Usually after tamely lobbing a medicine ball at each other for an hour, we'd be straight down the Bat & Ball opposite for the ground for a pint of Old Peculiar and the dish of the day. In the early days it was a common occurrence for the likes of Kevin Jarvis, Graham Dilley and Derek Underwood to enthusiastically slide down a couple of bitters before we ambled over to nets in the afternoon. These days, the counties won't stomach those sorts of antics and cricketers are put through their paces far more intensively. The appliance of science has seen us hooked up to more gadgetry than the Six Million Dollar Man and our weight and fitness levels are now measured electronically and closely scrutinised by the men in the white track-suits. If the boffins deemed you to be overweight, you'd immediately find yourself on a diet and, if the pounds went on instead of off, you'd be fined.

The advent of dieticians and sports psychologists may sound twee, but it has definitely extended many players' careers. While cricket may not appear as physically demanding as other major sports, the necessity to be able to concentrate for long periods of time in seventy degree heat requires a great deal of both stamina and mental athleticism. It could be argued that today's coaches are taking their fitness fixation a bench-press too far and are over-emphasizing training. I believe that while there is definitely a place for supreme fitness in a cricketer's make-up, first and foremost mental strength should be allied to sound technique. We're not athletes, we're cricketers and, at Kent, I thought that occasionally the campaign to turn us all into bat-waving Charles Atlases went a little too far. If you take a player like Martin McCague for example, his "fighting weight" is probably a stone heavier than the fitness police would like. However, if you bring him down from seventeen stone to sixteen, I believe you forfeit some of his natural strength and power. The experts therefore need to temper their approach with a little more realism. The scientific formulae they apply are a useful guide to a player's optimum fitness level, but by no means an infallible measure. For proof that there's no legislating for a player's metabolism you need look no further than Alan Ealham. Alan's legendary appetite (epitomised by his enthusiasm for the odd late-night cow pie) in no way negated the exemplary technique that made him the finest outfielder ever to grace the Kent ranks.

That said, the fitness culture over the past decade has prompted the vast improvement that has been seen in the standard of fielding. In the old days, we'd always carry two or three fielders, but now we wouldn't be able to hide a Kevin Jarvis or a Derek Underwood. As the influence and importance of one-day cricket has increased, every position - even third man or fine leg - is a vital one in its own right.

I do nevertheless believe that the overall standards of batting and bowling have fallen over the course of my career. When I first started, overseas players were very much part of the second team set-up and week-in, week-out, allowing the fringe players the chance to hone their game against some top-quality performers. Nowadays, while we still have some very fine young cricketers, the middle ground is overpopulated with some pretty average players who are doing little more than just ticking over in their own particular comfort zone. And the reason for this comparative lethargy? Quite simply, county cricket in its present form has turned into an anachronism and, more disconcertingly, it's no fun any more.

Having haemorrhaged spectators at a break-neck rate over the last two decades, the championship game does indeed face a worryingly uncertain future. Sadly, if the current rate of attrition is maintained, the players out in the middle will shortly outnumber the paying public. I'd surmise that the championship has in fact attracted no new spectators whatsoever over the last twenty years and what we are now experiencing is the gradual and ultimately terminal erosion of the die-hard core.

The key word is "boredom". In the 1997 edition of *The Cricketers' Who's Who* I condemned the seventeen match marathon that makes up the County Championship as being 'generally very tedious...boredom bores me.' Graham Cowdrey also aired his concerns: 'I feel an underlying depression is quietly destroying the game. It's time for everyone, and that includes the media, the players and the clubs to be more positive and optimistic.'

The principal reason for its demise is that while other popular sports, especially football, have almost reinvented themselves in the pursuit of a new audience, the county game remains stubbornly entangled in its conservative roots. If you looked at the first division of the football league in 1980, you'd have seen an unsponsored, underfunded, underattended, clapped-out product that was being held to ransom by burgeoning hooliganism and dilapidated stadia. Though its subsequent metamorphosis has not been perhaps to the taste of every grass-roots supporter, football is now a "must-have" premium brand. Club chairmen and the FA cleverly tapped into the football mania unleashed by Gazza's exploits at Italia '90 and turned the new Premiership into the most successful and exciting league in the world.

Without a similar fundamental reappraisal of how our game is marketed, county cricket is in danger of condemning itself to sporting oblivion. The administrators may try to comfort themselves that the game's ingrained on the national psyche and therefore cannot die, but if cricket allows football the opportunity to encroach further into its five month summer window, it risks losing its status as a major national sport altogether.

Bussing in hordes of flagpole saluting marketing men to rip the soul out of the game is not the solution. That said, the key to regenerating cricket must be to broaden its appeal by offering new supporters a more exciting and dynamic product. The average age of a member of a county cricket club is doubtless over fifty and this figure has to be reduced substantially if the game is to thrive or indeed have a future. If that means upsetting the traditionalists by changing a few rules, then so be it. Whether the new England & Wales Cricket Board has the will or gumption to redesign the way the game is played I am not so sure, but if it took time out to listen to the players for a change, it would be under no illusion whatsoever as to the parlous state of county cricket at the moment.

But let's at least concede that a start has been made. A two divisional county championship, a change I had suggested as far back as 1994, has certainly made a difference. From mid-season, too many cricketers had nothing to play for and, despite their professional pride, started to lose interest. But in 2000, the prospect of promotion and relegation at last gave teams the welcome kick up the backside they needed to finally motivate them all the way up to the finishing line. It is significant that in the first year of two divisions, there was only a handful of points covering the top five places in the second division. Finally players were getting the competitive edge they needed. It's just a shame that it didn't happen five years ago because now we could have been looking to take the game on to the next stage.

Ironically, the success of the new Sunday League format, with its garish cocktail of lights, coloured clothing and raucous musical accompaniments, has compounded the crisis that is engulfing championship cricket. By comparison to the new kid on the block, the four-day game looks even more staid, dull and lifeless than ever.

So what's to be done? I'm not for one minute advocating trying to overlay the razzmatazz of one-day cricket onto the championship format. Four-day cricket is all about the primeval battle of wits between the bowler and the batsman, pure and simple. Any move to dilute that confrontation with gimmicky bowling and fielding restrictions would be a retrograde step that would devalue the game as a whole. In one-day cricket, the rules are so heavily loaded in favour of the batsman that neither party stands to benefit. Rigidly enforced restrictions on line and length mean that bowlers are little more than purveyors of fodder for batmen to cart them over the top into the underpopulated expanses of the outfield. It's exciting to watch, but it's cricketing candy floss.

Instead, the authorities need to heed the lessons from other sports and attempt to involve the spectator more. Turn up to a cricket ground and the only optional enhancement to your enjoyment that you will be offered is a cushion to ease your poor buttocks which are about to be numbed by several hours of occasionally abject tedium. With no big screens at most county grounds and radio commentaries a rarity, spectators have no interaction or involvement in the game. If you are rummaging around at the bottom of your bag searching for that errant pickled egg when a wicket falls, tough luck!

So if we live, as we are told, in the "information age", what's to stop cricket taking a leaf out of rugby's book and offering spectators headsets that are linked up to the umpire? Sitting on the midwicket boundary is hardly the optimum angle for judging the merits of an LBW shout, so an explanation from the umpire outlining the reasons for his decision would significantly increase the supporter's appreciation of what was actually going on. Likewise, the use of a third umpire for every game would bring the spectator closer to the action. Waiting for the red or green light from the man in his mysterious little box is a neat device that can offer a rare nugget of tension, not to mention help eradicate howling errors.

The next stage would be to distil the County Championship down from its oversized complement of eighteen counties into nine regional teams. By extracting the crème de la crème from each county and pooling them in regional representative sides, it would make for far more exciting, quality competition and, with the best constantly playing the best, it would also feed quickly into a far more successful England team. Importantly, a cricketing premier league with just nine teams would mean a significant reduction in the amount of cricket played. Currently, with too much cricket breeding mediocrity, English batsmen know they can afford to fail because there'll always be another opportunity coming their way in two or three days' time. In South Africa or Australia, batmen's minds are focused by the fact that each knock might be the last innings they get for two or three *weeks*.

I can't see how the average cricket lover would be able to resist a format in which each region would be able to field almost a test strength team. County sides would still exist, but they would operate on a level similar to the second eleven set up at the moment and would be used as feeder teams into the elite stream.

The stagnation of the game has been reflected in the performances of the test side. Since the glory days of Mike Gatting's trouncing of the Australians in 1986/87, England have done little more than chalk up the occasional consolation amid a catalogue of ignominious series defeats. The vicious circle of the last ten to fifteen years has seen underachievement in the international area filter down into the domestic scene, which has in turn sabotaged our production line of world-class cricketers.

While I do believe that to an extent English players are soft and lack the necessary desire and commitment to win, I can't help thinking that, as a cricketing nation, we've been in one of those cyclical dips that all teams suffer at one stage or another. Australia went through it in the late seventies as the absence of the Packer rebels ripped the heart out of the side. It looks like the West Indies are now having to endure a similar crisis. The domination of Australia at the moment hasn't got anything to do with fancy academies and other such hokum. Sometimes a core of seven or eight world class players emerges and there's nothing the rest of the world can do about it. Just blame Mrs Waugh for having twins!

With luck, the consecutive series victories over Zimbabwe, the West Indies, Pakistan and Sri Lanka will help nudge England towards the broad, sunlit uplands of yesteryear. In Caddick, Gough, White and Cork, we at last seem to have unearthed a world-class bowling unit capable of bowling sides out twice. And if Atherton, Stewart and Thorpe keep free of injury and play close to their potential, the 2001 Ashes series will still be very much up for grabs.

With the new central contracts from the ECB, our key test players are now being sent the right sort of messages from the administrators. Too often, the constant chopping and changing by the selectors undermined England's cohesiveness as a unit. With such a huge pool of players from which to choose, the temptation has always been to experiment with an infinite number of variations until the nirvana of the perfect team blend is found. The number of one-test-wonders in the English game bears testament to the myopia of the selection policy and the precariousness of playing for the test side. At least with central contracts, players understand that they're established as part of the international set-up and are unlikely to be banished back to their counties after a single poor game, never to be seen or heard of again. Without a similar embarrassment of riches at their disposal, the Australian selectors have had to invest much more in each player's development, with the result that they have established a settled, yet robust, cricketing elite. Finally we seem to be learning their lessons.

While the Australian stars are cosseted like thoroughbreds, English players have traditionally been treated like shire horses. In the past, crucial players like Darren Gough will have finished a gruelling test match on a Monday, only to be thrust back into a four-day county game on the Wednesday. Sometimes they might even be plunged into an important Benson & Hedges or NatWest one-dayer on the Tuesday. This ludicrous situation has meant that England's premier strike bowler has been almost a permanent fixture on the treatment slab, with neither Yorkshire nor the test team ever getting any real degree of consistency out of him. At least with central contracts, the ECB has the right to rest players as it sees fit, thus sparing them the attrition of yet another round of matches. It may not suit the counties, but the peace of mind and sense of inclusiveness that central contracts have offered the top echelon of players has, in my mind, helped England start to turn the corner.

No matter what fancy systems the selectors employ, they will always have to trust to luck regarding the emergence of new talent. Fortunately at the moment I believe there's plenty of new young potential stars waiting in the wings. I particularly like the look of the Northamptonshire batsman David Sales. When he gets in and scores runs, he's got the hunger, desire and concentration to score *big* runs. In my book a natural test player should be able to grind relentlessly on and show the necessary patience and application to turn a century into 150 and then a double ton. Gooch and Atherton could do it and I think Sales may have the right blend of talent and temperament to join them.

Let's just hope that if he does get his chance, he's left alone by the media to play his own game. David takes a little bit of flak over his fitness and it would be a pity if his natural ability is diminished by some media witch-hunt over his weight. The totally unnecessary persecution that Andrew Flintoff suffered due to his extra poundage is sadly typical of some newspapers' perpetual determination to eliminate the positive and accentuate the negative with all things England. Flintoff's got a good, confident attitude, so it baffles me why the press should be so keen to knock it out of him. At least he did manage to get his own back beautifully when he simply commented 'Not bad for a fat boy' when interviewed after winning man of the match in one of the one-day competitions.

On the bowling front, I believe Yorkshire's Matthew Hoggard has got what it takes to go all the way. Having burst onto the scene impressively in 1999, he's managed to do what so many other "discoveries" have failed to do in the past and maintain his excellent form into a second season. He's quick, bowls good line and length and swings it away, so he's got more than half a chance.

In my view these players not only have the talent, but also the necessary arrogance, to succeed in the game long term. They're also very much individuals, as opposed to the injection-moulded clones so coveted by England regimes of the recent past. If the coaches can, for once, resist trying to coach the natural exuberance out of these players, they'll stand a chance of unearthing a new David Gower rather than another Mark Ramprakash. I don't mean that disrespectfully to Ramps because he's a fine player. All I'm saying is that however technically adept you become as a batsman, there's no substitute for unbridled, natural flair.

Through most of my career, the ECB, or the TCCB as it was formerly, enjoyed a cosy, comfortable relationship with its broadcaster of choice, the BBC. When the rights to televise home test matches were lost to Channel Four, it jarred the sensibilities of the traditionalists who feared the status of the game was being dangerously downgraded by its migration to a lesbian-loving "minority interest" channel. Yet the truth is that their fears have been unfounded and Channel Four's innovative and imaginative approach has made a mockery of the Beeb's woefully pedestrian coverage over the last thirty years. The snickometer, the LBW "blue strip" and Simon Hughes' informative analysis have all proved to be clever restyling devices that have become immensely popular. Since monochrome gave way to colour in 1969, it's difficult to remember one single material enhancement made by the BBC to the way it televised cricket, with the possible exception of getting rid of Jack Bannister. The Corporation forgot that in this day and age, money talks and, with cricket underfunded at every level, bottom dollar will no longer do.

Channel Four's two other coups of note were to firstly choose a theme tune that was so catchy it elbowed its way past two dozen boy-bands and Britney to the number one spot and, secondly, it recruited the quality benchmark of all commentators, Richie Benaud. Sublime understatement is still his trademark, despite the creeping culture of commentary box hysteria, and plum LBW appeals will never be termed anything other than "very close". His mind is still at least half an over ahead of everyone else's.

Boycott apart, the BBC contingent were a soporific collection of has-beens who were never going to identify with the younger age groups that the game desperately needed to attract. Though the armchair fan has every right to complain about the intrusion of commercial breaks, in net terms I believe he's far better off with the Sky and Channel Four package. The imposition of racing on a Saturday afternoon is far more contentious and hopefully Channel Four will hold a stewards' enquiry and re-route it onto a digital channel when their current agreement expires. Not that it would bother me or some of the other boys too much though. Sitting in the pavilion, you can be seen to be watching Robert Croft grind his way through an over when all of a sudden it would be the 2.30 from Haydock Park. Heaven!

While I'm pleased that first-class cricket is gradually adopting more sophisticated and professional attitudes, I think club cricket desperately needs to take a step back and reappraise itself. Up and down the country, the grass roots of the game are withering as run-of-the-mill county league teams attempt to assert themselves as quasi-professional outfits with experimental formats, sponsored clothing and overseas players. Wander in at tea in some club grounds in Kent and it's almost like turning up at the Bay Side Diner in *Home & Away*!

The set up these days fails to bridge the gap between the club cricket and first-class cricket. Club sides are now packing their ranks with paid, and often fairly mediocre, overseas players and this is stunting the development of young local talent. Promising youngsters, who would have normally progressed through their local colts set up, can't now get the exposure to a higher standard of cricket in the county league because some hulking great galah from New South Wales on a six month shagging holiday has nicked his spot for £100 a week! Bars in London can't get any staff any more as they're all down here opening the bowling.

So if the Kent league sides think they're improving the overall standard of the county game by importing paid overseas players, they're sadly mistaken. Most of them are between twenty-five and thirty and are never going to make it in professional cricket. Talented sixteen or seventeen-year-olds should be playing division one Kent League cricket, but they're just not getting the opportunity. In an ideal world, they would develop and show enough progress over two or three years for them to be in a position to play second team county cricket by the time they're twenty-one. In the current situation, players aren't making it into the fringes of the county scene until twenty-three or twenty-four, and that's too late.

I speak candidly on this subject, even though I'm currently one of those hired guns myself. On Saturdays I turn out in the Kent League for Gore Court, a Sittingbourne club for whom I played a season back in 1978. While I've been drafted in primarily to score top order runs, I also see it as part of my remit to try and offer coaching and advice on life as a first-class cricketer for younger players with those sorts of aspirations. If it was a just a case of me turning up, smacking a quick fifty and picking up my money, I couldn't help but regard myself as a co-signatory of the club's eventual death warrant.

Unfortunately, another questionable move was the Kent League's decision to string out matches over two consecutive weekends. Because the South Africans and the Australians have adopted this curious format and appear successful, the league decided to make a hasty leap onto the bandwagon. What they didn't realise is that everything that glitters isn't necessarily green and gold and that in local league terms the format was a complete non-starter. Clubs were jobbed into agreeing the change by a financial inducement after the Kent League board found some sponsorship. As soon as cash was mentioned, the clubs piled in without really examining what they were getting themselves into. In my view the league has constructed a rather unsightly edifice on what should be the breeding ground of Kent cricket.

The new model does nothing for the players' enjoyment of the game either. Let's not forget that club cricket is essentially a weekend leisure activity for young guys with regular jobs. Under the one innings per weekend system, you may open the batting and be unlucky enough to get a first-baller on the opening Saturday. You would then have no involvement at all in the rest of the day's play and, if you didn't bowl, all you'd have to look forward to for the following Saturday would be a riveting three sessions in the field. It's hardly surprising then that plenty of club cricketers are hankering for a return to the old format.

The administrators need to get things like this right because the game is being choked off at its roots. With schools cricket virtually non-existent, the ECB needs to get its message across to the generation for whom cricket is a hardly-used option on their Playstations and little else. Kwik Cricket, a happy-clappy facsimile of the game for the under tens, is a nice piece of window-dressing, but it's only the gentlest of introductions to the sport. Without doubt the ECB needs to flood the schools with players and youth development officers and really sell the game as if it were a brand new concept. I shudder to think how many Viv Richardses and Ian Bothams have never picked up a bat or held a ball because nobody had given them the opportunity. Club cricket is the only base from which tomorrow's county cricketers are going to develop. It's got to be given a chance.

Coming back down a couple of pegs to play in the Kent League for Gore Court and the Kent Village League for Stockbury, I've certainly discovered what a leveller club cricket really is. In county cricket, even so-called "poor" wickets spoil a batsman. By comparison, Stockbury's little strip of horrors, and I beg the groundsman's pardon, resembles Port Stanley runway after the Vulcans had been at it. With the odds stacked so steeply in his favour, all your local village pieman has to do is plop one of his steak and kidney puddings in the general direction of the stumps and then stand back and wait as either a crack, a weed, a stone, a ridge, a patch of sump oil or golf club divot mark does his dirty work for him.

Most clubs haven't got a roller heavy enough to crush a packet of crisps and watering responsibilities are usually left firmly in the hands of mother nature. Batting can therefore quickly turn into an exercise of extra sensory perception. Get somebody genuinely sharp on some of these tracks and vaguely amusing inconsistency can instantly become a twenty-two yard death zone, a fact recognised by the tacit acceptance at village level that helmets are now not merely the garb of sissies and show ponies!

In their own way, the innocuous slow-medium tweak merchants of the Bethersdens, Bordens and Bredgars of this world are just as much of a challenge as facing a Shane Warne or a Malcolm Marshall. If you're sensing that I'm starting to bleat a little bit too much mitigation, you'd be right! Despite predicting a shed load of runs for myself, I only managed to average just over thirty playing for Stockbury in 2000, a tiny premium on my first-class average of 28. I'm not sure it was the type of pillaging that my skipper Nigel had in mind when he asked me to swap my annual presentation evening duties for a berth at the top of the order. I'm still waiting nervously by the 'phone for this season's call!

Despite the state of the wickets, and being on a hiding to nothing, my season with Stockbury was good fun and it was pleasing that so many of the opposition players appeared to enjoy finding a county player in the ranks. I find it comical that if a village side brings in a second rate Aussie or a South African, there's normally a mutiny, but if they enlist a former county skipper, everything's suddenly sweetness and light!

The milk of human kindness was nevertheless curiously absent from some of my appearances in the more aggressively contested

Kent League. It's amazing how much these belligerent club cricketers want to get stuck into you and I quickly appreciated that I was public enemy number one in most of the games I played. What these club wannabees with attitude failed to realise, however, was that over the course of twenty years I'd managed to withstand a level of verbal and physical battering that most of these weekend wonders couldn't even begin to imagine.

I'd always had a reputation for having a few things to say for myself out on a cricket field and in a match away against Sydenham, it was just like stepping back into the old routine. Sydenham were batting and their number three snicked one to first slip, didn't walk, but was given out. Off he went. Then their captain came in and very soon edged one from our spinner through to the 'keeper (I was fielding in the in-field at the time). Once again the Sydenham batsman stood his ground, but this time our umpire didn't raise his finger. It was a blatant edge and our 'keeper walked past him at the end of the over and asked him whether he hit it. The batsman admitted he had, but added that it wasn't his decision to make. Fair enough, "that's boxing", as Frank Bruno no doubt would have said, and we got on with the game.

After tea I went out to open our reply and it was pretty clear they regarded me as the "big wicket". It certainly wasn't going to be easy as the track was at best variable and they had a pretty useful West Indian opening bowler. Then, as so often is the way, I lost concentration and knicked a big one behind off the bloke from the other end. Presuming that we would probably struggle if I got out early, I decided to try my luck and hang around for the decision. It was indeed my lucky day as our umpire gave me not out, much to the disbelief and wrath of the opposition. Of course it all then went off and abuse came flying in at me from all directions. For a while I just sat on my bat and said nothing, but as the bowlers lost their composure, I started to give a bit back. The infuriated West Indian lost the plot for two or three overs and started bowling short. I gleefully pulled him for several fours, flapping him back a sarcastic yawn each time the ball fizzed through mid-wicket.

Then we came off for rain and, after another tetchy dispute over the fact that they hadn't put the covers on, I persuaded the guys that at 110 for 1, we should go back out and chase the target of 180-odd we needed to win. After I'd advised the opposition that sledging me would be about as effective as trying to dent the *Bismarck* with a spud-gun, we eventually recommenced our innings. For a while everyone got on with the game and it all seemed to quieten down again. Then our number three sent a big edge through to their 'keeper and, you guessed it, didn't walk. In a sphincter-puckering moment he was given not out by our umpire.

Given what had gone on before, it was obviously too much for five of the opposition and they just walked off the field in disgust. Up came the stumps and it was all over. We had a few youngsters in our side and a couple of them were pretty apprehensive at having to run a possible gauntlet of peeved Sydenham players out of the changing-room back to the sanctuary of the car park. So I went into the opposition dressing-room for a word and approached their captain.

'Just two things. Your number three knicked it to slip and didn't walk. You knicked one to the keeper and didn't walk and weren't given out by our umpire...'

'How do you know that?'

'Well I asked my wicket-keeper and you told him.'

'Yeah, you're right, I knicked it but didn't walk.'

'Well that's double standards. It's OK for you to stand there but it's not OK for me to stand there..'

'Yeah, yeah, but we knew we had to get you out...'

'No, it's irrelevant who I am. You can't play by these rules, that's it.'

As I walked out I heard four or five of them get stuck in to the ones who had walked off saying 'he's dead right, you can't do this sort of thing...'

So all in all it made for a rather exciting Saturday afternoon in south London. As a footnote to the game, Gore Court were awarded the match with maximum points. Sydenham were later deducted twenty points by the league for abandoning the game, a punishment that sent them spiralling to the bottom of the league and subsequent relegation.

It's a great shame, though, that people's weekend recreation should so often degenerate into an atmosphere of the sort of pent-up stress, angst and "rage" sport is there to relieve. First-class cricketers have the advantage of living with pressure day in, day out. It's what professional sport is all about and the successful practitioners thrive on it. It's a pity the amateurs these days have to take themselves so seriously.

For me, my enjoyment of cricket wasn't based solely on what occurred between eleven o'clock to stumps on match days. I loved the whole experience: playing the game, after the game, pre-season, the lot. It was a lovely sport to be involved in. I met some great people, not only in cricket but from all walks of life, and had the opportunity to do things and see places that simply weren't on the radar for most conventional forms of employment.

Yet from 1998, a little bit of passion started to ebb from the love affair. It wasn't anything to do with losing the captaincy or the sands of time catching up with my aching limbs, it was more that the predictability of my annual routine was finally taking its toll. The old enthusiasm was starting to wane and, when I started to pull open the curtains in the morning half hoping to see rain clouds, I knew something had changed.

While I still loved batting, it was the 'keeping that was beginning to drag me down. It was getting to the stage where I'd be travelling to the ground in the morning almost dreading the prospect of being out in the field all day. However, once I got out into the middle, I was fine. I'd always been able to motivate myself and my body just seemed to click over into auto-pilot. I was a natural born competitor, and that battling quality, like a boxer's punch, would always be the last attribute I'd lose. With Paul Nixon now first choice 'keeper, there seemed no reason to alter my long-term plan of retiring when my contract expired at the end of the 2000 season. I knew I wouldn't be keeping wicket, so I threw myself into my batting, hoping that my reputation as a gritty middle order accumulator might be enough to sneak me back into the first team. As it turned out, I did get my last hurrah as Matthew Fleming called on my not insubstantial Sunday League nous to help negotiate the team away from the division one drop-zone.

Shortly before Kent's final home CGU National League match I formally announced my retirement from first-class cricket. Playing Yorkshire in Kent's first game under floodlights at Canterbury had to be the perfect stage on which to bid my farewells. Sad to say, I only got 14, but from the volume of the standing ovation I received it could have been 314. I'm not in any way an emotional person, but if there was ever to be an occasion when a tear could have forced its way into my tired old sentimental eye, then that would have been it!

The curtain came down for the final time the following Sunday at Worcester. Pleasingly, the match was far from dead rubber. Worcestershire were fighting it out with us at the bottom of the league and the match was in effect a final eliminator for division one survival. Winners stayed up, losers went down, and Sky TV were there for the showdown. Worcester batted first and, on a ropey end of season wicket, were bowled out for just over a hundred. With the ball seaming around all over the place and the world's best bowler, Glenn McGrath, revved up and raring, there was still plenty of cricket left to be played.

I concluded with my fellow opener, Dave Fulton, that the only way Worcester were going to win was if McGrath started to run amok. We battened down the hatches and, with the Australian bowling to six slips, counted survival as our lone priority. Fortunately the ploy paid off and it wasn't long before McGrath was loping his wicketless way back to the boundary and we were moving smoothly towards our target. As the winning-post started to come into view, I started to loosen up and play some shots. Then, on 32, a juicy slow left-armer named Matthew Rawnsley came on and, with a lick of the lips, I gave him the charge and, bosh, dumped him out the ground for six! Hungry for a bit more glory, I went for a gallop after the next ball only to miss it by a mile and get bowled. It would have been nice if I could have strolled up the wicket, said a couple of goodbyes and allowed myself to be stumped, but that would have been too perfect. However I consoled myself with the fact that I'd seen off the world's best bowler, hit my last scoring shot for six, helped save Kent from relegation and even won "man of the match" for the first time ever in a Sunday League game. Considering it was all on live TV, there's got to be worse ways to end your career!

Once I did make the decision to retire, I thought I'd probably enjoy a honeymoon period for four or five months and then start to hanker for the day-to-day involvement and the camaraderie. I've got to say, however, that as I write in March 2001, I'm missing it like a grouse misses August 12th. There's no more fretting about getting 13.3 on the bleep test or running the 20 metre sprint in three seconds, let alone the number of runs or catches I'm going to get next season. I feel content that the time was obviously right and I am now looking forward to relaunching my career in my new post with the Professional Cricketers' Association. In amplifying the voice, and hopefully the influence, of professional cricketers, the PCA performs a function that has always been close to my heart. It's probably a life's work trying to alter the mind-set of some of the dinosaurs that run our game, but it's an undertaking I'm determined to tackle in typical Marsh fashion: direct and uncompromising.

Looking back, it will always rankle that I didn't win more trophies with Kent and missed out on playing for England. Everyone likes the limelight and I feel a little cheated that I never got the profile that my ability and potential, in my view, deserved. We're all driven by vanity and insecurity in varying measures and I have to admit I feel a more than a little irked that I never really got my place in the sun. If I'd got that England spot, I wouldn't have let it go, no way.

It would be churlish to carp too loudly. I had a wonderful career in most respects and have achieved, trophies aside, about as much as I could ever have dreamed at county level. A world record, 668 catches, 61 stumpings and over 10,000 runs in 291 first-class matches wasn't a bad return for somebody who hadn't even set eyes on a set of stumps until he was 14! I've been lucky in so many ways, but particularly in the unqualified support of my family. My cause has always been championed by Julie who, fortunately for me, was born into a cricketing family and was fully aware of the pitfalls of the lifestyle. Despite being the archetypal cricket widow, Julie's always stood by me and never questioned anything I did. I couldn't ask any more than that. Even my two children, Hayley, who's now fourteen, and Christian, ten, empathised with their father's rather unorthodox profession. Christian always showed an appreciation beyond his tender years, while Hayley, who never enjoyed watching me play, was nevertheless always thoughtful enough to pop a good luck note in my pocket before I went away for a big game. My family realised that professional sportsmen have to be selfish at times, yet the encouragement they offered me through thick and thin was one of the rocks on which the success of my career was built.

Our son's in the Kent Under 10 squad for the 2001 season and, after contemplating becoming a bowler, has decided to follow his pa into wicket-keeping. I know how difficult it was for Graham Cowdrey being the son and brother of celebrated cricketers. Admittedly, the Marsh name isn't quite in that bracket (yet!), but nevertheless comparisons with fathers and grandfathers are bound to be made. I'll give him all the support, encouragement and coaching he wants, but I've also made sure he knows it's not going to be easy. I can only keep my fingers crossed that the three lions of England will one day take an interest in our little Christian!

Steve Marsh Career Statistics

Up to and including the 2000 season.

Compiled by Howard Milton

FIRST-CLASS CRICKET

Against	Mtchs	Inns	N.O.	Runs	H.S.	Ave	100	50	Ct	St
Derbyshire	16	24	2	630	88	28.63	-	6	42	1
Durham	9	13	2	327	92	29.72	-	2	22	2
Essex	20	29	3	787	127	30.26	2	2	46	3
Glamorgan	15	19	3	325	72*	20.31	-	3	43	3
Gloucestershire	16	24	5	727	90*	38.26	-	7	43	5
Hampshire	19	27	3	535	73	22.29	-	4	57	6
Lancashire	16	22	1	592	78	28.19	-	5	29	4
Leicestershire	18	27	8	630	98*	33.15	-	4	45	8
Middlesex	20	31	5	698	108*	26.84	1	2	42	5
Northants	12	18	6	463	65	38.58	-	1	15	2
Nottinghamshire	13	23	3	541	114*	27.05	1	1	38	2
Somerset	14	23	4	447	113*	23.52	1	1	25	3
Surrey	19	30	3	514	67	19.03	-	2	39	2
Sussex	19	30	6	721	142	30.04	1	4	51	3
Warwickshire	16	25	3	443	70	20.13	-	3	38	2
Worcestershire	14	18	1	342	67*	20.11	-	3	30	5
Yorkshire	14	19	4	574	125	38.26	1	2	30	1
Cambridge Uni'	5	5	1	163	57	40.75	-	1	10	2
Oxford Uni'	5	4	2	188	100*	94.00	1	1	11	1
Australia	3	6	3	101	35*	33.66	-	-	13	-
India	2	2	1	65	44	65.00	-	-	1	1
Pakistan	1	2	-	29	28	14.50	-	-	-	-
South Africa	1	1	-	57	57	57.00	-	1	6	-
West Indies	2	4	-	45	22	11.25	-	-	9	-
Zimbabwe	1	1	-	111	111	111.00	1	-	-	-
Zimbabwe B	1	2	-	43	30	21.50	-	-	3	-
TOTAL	291	429	69	10,098	142	28.05	9	55	688	61

Season	Mtchs	Inns	N.O.	Runs	H.S.	Ave	100	50	Ct	St
1982	2	1	1	10	10*	-	-	-	6	-
1983	1	2	-	5	5	2.50	-	-	-	-
1984	5	7	1	106	48	17.66	-	-	11	-
1985	3	4	1	59	31*	19.66	-	-	9	3
1986	26	36	8	857	70	30.60	-	5	48	3
1987	21	27	5	411	72*	18.68	-	2	39	2
1988	23	25	6	713	120	24.58	2	1	56	5
1989	22	31	6	614	90*	24.56	-	5	40	1
1990	24	35	8	911	114*	33.74	1	5	49	5
1991	23	32	5	910	113*	33.70	2	5	66	4
1992	22	30	4	896	125	34.46	1	6	44	8
1993 (Zimbabwe Tour)	1	2	-	43	30	21.50	-	-	3	-
1993	19	27	2	667	111	26.68	1	4	57	4
1994	19	31	6	807	88	32.28	-	5	69	5
1995	16	28	3	688	67*	27.52	-	4	32	2
1996	15	24	1	478	127	20.78	1	2	28	6
1997	18	27	6	837	142	39.85	1	3	61	2
1998	16	28	4	620	92	25.83	-	5	42	4
1999	15	22	2	466	73*	23.30	-	2	28	7
TOTAL	291	429	69	10,098	142	28.05	9	55	688	61

N.B. Steve took two catches in four matches when he did not keep wicket.

Five dismissals in an innings.

ct st

8 - v. Middlesex, Lord's 1991
6 1 v. Durham, Canterbury 1994
5 1 v. Warwickshire, Folkestone 1986
6 - v. Leicestershire, Leicester 1991
6 - v. South Africa, Canterbury 1994
6 - v. Nottinghamshire, Nottingham 1997
5 - v. Australia, Canterbury 1985

ct st

5 4 1 v. Hampshire, Canterbury 1991
5 5 - v. Glamorgan, Canterbury 1992
5 5 - v. Gloucestershire, Cheltenham 1994
5 4 1 v. Essex, Canterbury 1995
5 5 - v. Australia, Canterbury 1997
5 5 - v. Hampshire, Canterbury 1998
5 5 - v. Gloucestershire, Bristol 1998

Steve is the only wicket-keeper to take more than six dismissals in an innings for Kent, a feat he achieved twice. His eight dismissals in an innings equalled the then world record. Uniquely he scored 108* in the same match. The eight catches are still a world record.

Seven dismissals in a match.

ct st			ct st		
9 9 -	v.	Middlesex, Lord's 1991	7 7 -	v.	Nottinghamshire, Nottingham 1997
9 8 1	v.	Durham, Canterbury 1994	7 7 -	v.	Australia, Canterbury 1997
7 7 -	v.	Hampshire, Bournemouth 1988	7 7 -	v.	Hampshire, Canterbury 1998
7 6 1	v.	Hampshire, Canterbury 1991			
7 6 1	v.	Glamorgan, Canterbury 1991			
7 6 1	v.	Worcestershire, Canterbury 1994			
7 6 1	v.	Somerset, Canterbury 1994			

Steve's nine catches in a match is a Kent record shared with Jack Hubble and Alan Knott.

Steve's 749 dismissals in his first-class career for Kent places him fourth on the all-time list of Kent wicket-keepers. But if catches taken by Les Ames when not keeping wicket are excluded, Steve is the third behind Fred Huish (1253) and Alan Knott (915).

Steve has taken the most dismissals in a season for Kent since the first-class programme was reduced in 1969: 74 (69 ct, 5 st) in 1994.

Steve holds the Kent record for keeping in the highest innings total ever made against Kent not to include a bye: 559 by Surrey (Canterbury) 1995.

Dismissals off Kent bowlers
(all caught unless otherwise specified)

87 M. J. McCague	17 T. A. Merrick	2 G. R. Dilley
86 A. P. Igglesden	12 K. B. S. Jarvis	2 G. J. Johnson
55 M. V. Fleming	12 B. J. Phillips	2 (st 2) L. Potter
51 (st 19) R. P. Davies	12 R. F. Pienaar	2 N. W. Preston
51 (st 19) M. M. Patel	10 T. N. Wren	2 (st 1) A. Symonds
49 D. W. Headley	9 (st 4) D. L. Underwood	2 (st 1) C. J. Tavare
47 C. Penn	8 (st 3) M. D. Harman	1 M. R. Benson
44 M. A. Ealham	8 (st 1) P. A. Strang	1 S. G. Hinks
42 R. M. Ellison	7 D. J. M. Kelleher	1 D. A. Scott
22 T. M. Alderman	5 P. S. de Villiers	1 G.D. Spelman
22 (st 2) C. S. Cowdrey	4 H. L. Alleyne	1 D. J. Spencer
21 (st 1) J. B. D. Thompson	3 (St 2) N. J. Llong	1 (st 1) E. J. Stanford
20 E. A. E. Baptiste	3 V. J. Wells	1 T. R. Ward
20 (st 5) C. L. Hooper	2 G. R.Cowdrey	1 R. A. Woolmer

FIRST-CLASS CRICKET (cont.)

Hundreds (9)

142 v. Sussex, Horsham 1997
127 v. Essex, Ilford 1996
125 v. Yorkshire, Canterbury 1992
120 v. Essex, Chelmsford 1988
114* v. Notts, Tunbridge Wells 1990

113* v. Somerset, Taunton 1991
111 v. Zimbabwe, Canterbury 1993
108* v. Middlesex, Lords 1991
100* v. Oxford University, Oxford 1988

Steve also scored **98*** v. Leicestershire (Canterbury) 1997, the highest ever score by a Kent batsman at number 9 in the order.

Hundred Partnerships (17)

235†	6th	G. R. Cowdrey	v.	Yorkshire, Canterbury 1992
222†	7th	G. R. Cowdrey	v.	Essex, Chelmsford 1988
183†	10th	B. J. Phillips	v.	Sussex, Horsham 1997
166†	7th	D. J. Spencer	v.	Zimbabwe, Canterbury 1993
162*	6th	C. S. Cowdrey	v.	Glamorgan, Canterbury 1987
150	7th	J. B. D. Thompson	v.	Essex, Ilford 1996
150†	6th	A. P. Wells	v.	Durham, Canterbury 1998
146†	8th	M. A. Ealham	v.	Leicestershire, Canterbury 1997
139†	7th	M. A. Ealham	v.	Derbyshire, Derby 1994
137†	6th	G. R. Cowdrey	v.	Gloucestershire, Bristol 1992
126	7th	M. A. Ealham	v.	Sussex, Hove 1995
125†	6th	N. J. Llong	v.	Cambridge University, Cambridge 1993
122	7th	M. V. Fleming	v.	Gloucestershire, Canterbury 1999
115	7th	R. P. Davis	v.	Lancashire, Manchester 1992
113	6th	N. R. Taylor	v.	Glamorgan, Canterbury 1992
104	7th	C. S. Cowdrey	v.	Warwickshire, Folkestone 1986
100	7th	M. A. Ealham	v.	Lancashire, Lytham 1993

† denotes Kent record wicket partnership against the opponents concerned.

The 10th wicket partnership is the second highest in Kent history, exceeded only by F. E. Woolley and A. Fielder's English record partnership of 235 v. Worcestershire (Stourbridge) 1909.

The partnerships of 235 and 146 are also Kent record partnerships for the 6th and 8th wicket respectively at Canterbury.

Steve as a Bowler

Steve took two first-class wickets, both in an analysis of 2-20 v. Warwickshire (Birmingham) 1990, A. R. K. Pierson lbw b Marsh 6, A. A. Donald c Igglesden b Marsh 1.

Bowling for a declaration v. Glamorgan (Swansea) 1992, Steve conceded 34 runs (666646) in one over to Matthew Maynard, the most expensive over ever bowled in a Kent match.

SUNDAY LEAGUE/NATIONAL LEAGUE

Against	Mtchs	Inns	N.O.	Runs	H.S.	Ave	100	50	Ct	St
Derbyshire	12	8	2	114	30*	19.00	-	-	13	-
Durham	6	3	1	31	19	15.50	-	-	4	2
Essex	13	11	5	92	27*	15.33	-	-	15	-
Glamorgan	13	10	3	134	32	19.14	-	-	7	2
Gloucestershire	15	8	2	154	34	25.66	-	-	16	2
Hampshire	14	8	-	50	19	6.25	-	-	10	3
Lancashire	14	9	3	131	38	21.83	-	-	17	-
Leicestershire	15	13	7	200	59	33.33	-	1	15	-
Middlesex	12	8	1	144	53	20.57	-	1	16	-
Northamptonshire	12	9	2	138	52	19.71	-	1	9	-
Nottinghamshire	10	9	1	142	56	17.75	-	1	8	2
Somerset	12	8	3	113	40	22.60	-	-	19	4
Surrey	13	13	3	156	35	15.60	-	-	11	-
Sussex	13	8	2	87	36*	14.50	-	-	8	3
Warwickshire	14	10	4	102	24*	17.00	-	-	12	2
Worcestershire	15	8	3	109	38	21.80	-	-	9	3
Yorkshire	14	11	3	120	25	15.00	-	-	11	-
TOTAL	**217**	**154**	**45**	**2,017**	**59**	**18.50**	**-**	**4**	**200**	**23**

N.B. Steve made three catches in eight matches when he did not keep wicket.

Four dismissals in an innings.

ct	st		
5	5	-	v. Middlesex, Canterbury 1987
5	5	-	v. Lancashire, Manchester 1995
4	4	-	v. Lancashire, Manchester 1987
4	1	3	v. Sussex, Maidstone 1988
4	3	1	v. Somerset, Bath 1989
4	4	-	v. Lancashire, Folkestone 1989

Steve's five dismissals in an innings is the Kent record shared with Paul Downton and Alan Knott. His three stumpings in an innings is the Kent record shared with Alan Knott. His 223 dismissals (ct 200, st 23) (incl 3 caught in the field) is the Kent career record.

Dismissals off Kent bowlers
(all caught unless otherwise specified)

28	M. V. Fleming	4	D. J. M. Kelleher	1	V. J. Wells
22	A. P. Igglesden	3	(st 1) G. R. Cowdrey	1	T. N. Wren
20	M. A. Ealham	3	(st 2) N. J. Llong		
20	M. J. McCague	3	B. J. Phillips		Above includes one catch
17	D. W. Headley	3	R. F. Pienaar		each off D. D. Masters,
13	(st 9) R. P. Davis	3	(st 1) D. L. Underwood		M. M. Patel and M. J.
11	C. Penn	3	(st 1) T. R. Ward		Saggers while not keeping
10	R. M. Ellison	2	G. R. Dilley		wicket.
9	(st 1) C. S. Cowdrey	1	P. A. de Silva		
8	(st 5) C. L. Hooper	1	K. B. S. Jarvis		
8	J. B. D. Thompson	1	D. D. Masters		
7	E. A. E. Baptiste	1	M. J. Saggers		
6	T. A. Merrick	1	D. J. Spencer		
6	(st 2) M. M. Patel	1	(st 1) P. A. Strang		
5	H. L. Alleyne	1	A. Symonds		

Fifties (4)

59 v. Leicestershire, Canterbury 1991
56 v. Nottinghamshire, Nottingham 1991
53 v. Middlesex, Lord's 1989
52 v. Northamptonshire, Canterbury 1991

NATWEST TROPHY

Against	Mtchs	Inns	N.O.	Runs	H.S.	Ave	100	50	Ct	St
Derbyshire	2	1	-	26	26	26.00	-	-	3	-
Gloucestershire	1	1	-	0	0	0.00	-	-	1	-
Hampshire	3	3	1	21	13	10.50	-	-	3	-
Middlesex	3	3	1	42	24*	21.00	-	-	4	-
Nottinghamshire	1	1	-	1	1	1.00	-	-	2	-
Somerset	1	-	-	-	-	-	-	-	1	-
Surrey	1	1	-	15	15	15.00	-	-	1	-
Warwickshire	6	5	-	96	55	19.20	-	1	10	1
Scotland	1	-	-	-	-	-	-	-	-	-
Minor Counties	8	4	1	36	23	12.00	-	-	12	4
TOTAL	27	19	3	237	55	14.81	-	1	37	5

N.B. Steve made one catch in one match when he did not keep wicket.

Four dismissals in an innings.

  ct st
5 5   -   v. Buckinghamshire, Canterbury 1988

Dismissals off Kent bowlers
(all caught unless otherwise specified)

5 R. M. Ellison	**2** (st 1) G. R. Cowdrey
5 D. W. Headley	**2** R. P. Davis
4 M. A. Ealham	**2** (st 2) N. J. Llong
4 M. J. McCague	**2** C. Penn
4 R. F. Pienaar	**2** (st 1) N. R. Taylor
3 M. V. Fleming	**1** E. A. E. Baptiste
3 A. P. Igglesden	**1** C. S. Cowdrey

1 J. B. D. Thompson
1 (st 1) T. R. Ward
Above includes one catch
off M. A. Ealham while not
keeping wicket.

Fifty (1)

71 v. Lancashire, Manchester 1991.

Steve as a Bowler

Steve took one wicket in an analysis of 1-0 v. Cambridgeshire (March) 1996
D. F. Ralfs c Preston b Marsh 6.

BENSON & HEDGES CUP

Against	Mtchs	Inns	N.O.	Runs	H.S.	Ave	100	50	Ct	St
Derbyshire	2	1	-	3	3	3.00	-	-	-	-
Essex	3	2	1	58	41*	58.00	-	-	5	-
Glamorgan	5	2	-	44	29	14.66	-	-	2	-
Gloucestershire	5	5	2	51	27	17.00	-	-	5	-
Hampshire	5	4	2	40	17*	20.00	-	-	6	-
Lancashire	2	2	-	75	71	37.50	-	1	2	-
Leicestershire	2	2	1	23	23*	23.00	-	-	2	-
Middlesex	5	4	1	42	15	14.00	-	-	8	-
Northamptonshire	4	4	1	57	27*	19.00	-	-	5	-
Nottinghamshire	2	2	-	38	26	19.00	-	-	3	-
Somerset	4	4	3	47	27	47.00	-	-	9	-
Surrey	8	6	2	86	37*	21.50	-	-	8	2
Sussex	4	2	-	6	4	3.00	-	-	7	2
Warwickshire	3	2	-	18	9	9.00	-	-	2	-
Worcestershire	3	3	1	44	24	22.00	-	-	4	-
Yorkshire	1	1	-	0	0	0.00	-	-	1	-
Universities	4	1	-	8	8	8.00	-	-	8	2
Ireland	1	-	-	-	-	-	-	-	-	-
Minor Counties	1	1	-	1	1	1.00	-	-	-	-
TOTAL	**64**	**48**	**14**	**641**	**71**	**18.85**	**-**	**1**	**77**	**6**

Four dismissals in an innings.

	ct	st	
4	4	-	v. Somerset, Maidstone 1996
4	3	1	v. British Universities, Oxford 1998

Dismissals off Kent bowlers
(all caught unless otherwise specified)

10	M. J. McCague	4	C. S. Cowdrey	2	E. A. E. Baptiste
9	M. A. Ealham	4	T. N. Wren	2	G. R. Dilley
8	(st 1) M. V. Fleming	3	(st 1) R. P. Davis	2	D. J. M. Kelleher
7	C. Penn	3	(st 2) M. M. Patel	2	(st 1) D. L. Underwood
6	R. M. Ellison	3	B. J. Phillips	1	C. L. Hooper
5	D. W. Headley	3	J. B. D. Thompson	1	T. A. Merrick
5	A. P. Igglesden	2	H. L. Alleyne	1	(st 1) P. A. Strang

Fifty (1)

55 v. Warwickshire, Birmingham 1995.
In making this fifty Steve shared with Dean Headley the Kent record partnership for the 9th wicket: 49.

England 'A'

Steve played in two limited-over matches for England 'A' v. Sri Lanka in 1991, scoring 26* and 28* and taking three catches.

Steve as Captain

Steve is one of only six Kent wicket-keepers to captain Kent in a match. He is the only one to be officially appointed Captain of Kent.

Playing record as Captain

	P	W	L	D/ND
First-Class matches 1991-98	69	26	22	21
Sunday/National League 1991-98	64	40	19	5
NatWest Trophy 1995-97	4	1	3	
Benson & Hedges Cup	22	15	6	1